QUESTION AND ANSWER GUIDE

AS/A-Level
General Studies

Second Edition

Colin Swatridge

Philip Allan Updates
Market Place
Deddington
Oxfordshire
OX15 0SE

tel: 01869 338652
fax: 01869 337590
e-mail: sales@philipallan.co.uk
www.philipallan.co.uk

© Philip Allan Updates 1999
Second edition 2002
This book was first published as part of the Exam Success Guide series. It has been revised and updated in accordance with the AS/A-Level specifications.

ISBN 0 86003 777 0

All rights reserved; no part of this publication may be reproduced, stored in a retrieval system, or transmitted, in any form or by any means, electronic, mechanical, photocopying, recording or otherwise without either the prior written permission of Philip Allan Updates or a licence permitting restricted copying in the United Kingdom issued by the Copyright Licensing Agency Ltd, 90 Tottenham Court Road, London W1P 9HE.

Cover illustration by John Spencer

Printed by Raithby, Lawrence & Co Ltd, Leicester

Contents

Introduction 1

Section 1: Document response
About this section 6

Arts	What is art?	8
	Media violence	13
	The literary canon	19
Social sciences	Gender bias	28
	Ethical foreign policy	32
	Social class	39
Sciences	Air pollution and asthma	47
	Transgenic pigs	52
	Obesity	58

Section 2: Data response
About this section 68

Arts	Listening and viewing hours	69
	The world's most highly priced paintings	72
Social sciences	The family in Britain	76
	The ageing process	79
	Economic status by gender and ethnicity	82
Sciences	Infectious diseases	86
	Carbon emissions	89

Section 3: Essays
About this section 94

Arts	Architecture	96
	The arts and public money	99
	Censorship	102
	Popular music	105
Social sciences	Religion and moral values	108
	Comprehensive schooling	111
	Trial by jury	114
	Our duty to vote	117
Sciences	Electrically powered rail transport	120
	Scientifically modified food	123
	Renewable energy	126
	Computer technology	129

Introduction

General Studies is not a subject like any others. It has no one corpus of knowledge and no one method of adding to knowledge or testing it. It tries to do a bit of everything, in the belief that (a) ultimately, knowledge is indivisible and (b) everyone should be something of a generalist as well as something of a specialist.

Each of the specifications of the A-level examining boards is different from the others. A book that tried to represent all the topics that might figure in a General Studies examination would be impossibly big and unwieldy. I did not want to write a big book, and you — the user — would not have wanted to plough through it if I had.

What I have done is to give some examples of each of the main question forms on General Studies papers: document-response questions, data-response questions and 'long' essays. In fact, examples of short, medium-length and longer essays are provided in each of these sections, since — though the word 'essay' may not be used — a piece of continuous prose is still required in answer to a large number of examination questions.

Students might not have contemplated doing any pre-examination revision of General Studies before — and, indeed, there is not a lot that can usefully be done. It is one of the beauties of General Studies that it is not a content-driven, learn-and-regurgitate subject. This book is, therefore, intended to be of use as much during an AS or A2 course as it is at the pre-examination stage — and it is intended to be of use as much to teachers of General Studies as it is to students.

General Studies is not about facts. Facts are merely the raw material of this subject — and you may well be presented with all the facts you need on the examination paper. General Studies is about the interpretation of facts, the marshalling of facts and the sorting of facts, ideas and opinions. Doing these things effectively comes with practice — and this practice can be had in General Studies lessons, in all other A-level lessons, in working through a book like this and by regular reading of:
- a selection of articles in Philip Allan magazines and, in particular, *Geography Review*, *Politics Review*, and *Sociology Review*;
- a broadsheet newspaper, like the *Guardian* or the *Independent* (and especially its various tabloid and magazine supplements);
- short articles from the weeklies (the *New Scientist*, *The Economist*, the *New Statesman*) of the sort that are used in exam questions.

Assessment Objectives

All General Studies examiners use the same criteria when marking. These are known as 'Assessment Objectives'. Examiners are required (by the government Qualifications and Curriculum Authority) to assess candidates' ability to:

Introduction

1 Demonstrate relevant knowledge and understanding applied to a range of issues, using skills from different disciplines (AO1).
2 Communicate clearly and accurately in a concise, logical and relevant way (AO2).
3 Marshal evidence and draw conclusions; select, interpret, evaluate and integrate information, data, concepts and opinions (AO3).
4 Demonstrate understanding of different types of knowledge and of the relationship between them, appreciating their limitations (AO4).

General Studies candidates have always been required to have a certain bedrock knowledge — to know something about the reasons for climate change; about the British political system; about different art-forms, and so on. They have also been expected to have a grasp of significant contemporary issues, like the threat and promise of genetic engineering, and the travails of our transport system. So AO1 has always been important. General Studies has a core subject content like any other subject, and candidates need to know and understand it.

There is nothing new about AO2 and 3 either. A sound level of English has always been required, and it always will be (AO2). The same goes for putting an argument together: assembling evidence, choosing among relevant items of information, integrating facts and opinions, and coming to a reasoned conclusion (AO3). Although AO3 still earns most marks, AO4 is new, and for this reason it is given some prominence here.

The overall weighting for the four Assessment Objectives is something like this:

Assessment Objective:	1	25%
	2	15%
	3	35%
	4	25%

You could probably earn 'pass' marks in the examination — you could even do quite well — if you show knowledge and understanding, put a decent argument together, and use the language competently. For high marks, though, you will need to meet AO4, so this deserves a closer look.

Assessment Objective 4 (AO4)

'Different types of knowledge' is perhaps best understood as 'different ways of getting knowledge'. Take the following examples:
- A mathematician gets it by calculation.
- A physicist gets it by measurement, and experiment.
- A biologist gets it by careful observation.
- A sociologist gets it by sampling and data-gathering.
- A historian gets it by inspecting documents and material remains.
- An artist gets it by drawing on feelings and experiences.

All these investigators have a range of ways of getting knowledge; but all depend on evidence of some sort. The evidence available to the physical scientist is likely to be quite *hard* — that is, it can be precisely measured; the scientist can be quite *objective* about it, and the conclusions reached can amount almost to *certainty*.

The historian or the philosopher may only have *soft* evidence to base their conclusions on, in the form of ideas, witness-statements, and diary-entries. It may not be possible to be objective about such evidence. A theologian or poet may actually rejoice in their *subjective* opinions. Whereas economists may admit that their projections give them no more than *probable* knowledge, and thinkers in the humanities may be quite content with what is *possibly* the case.

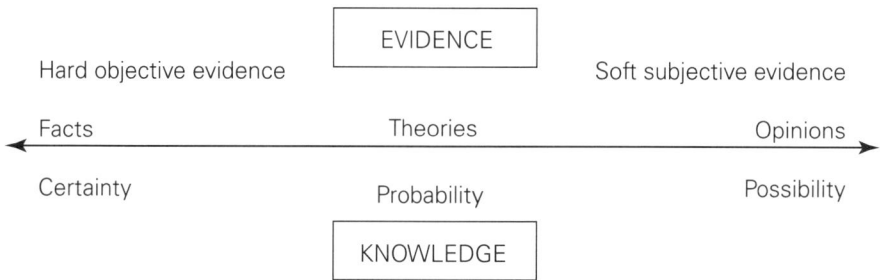

What does all this mean for General Studies? It means that we accept that knowledge is a matter of degree; that some knowledge will be a matter of *opinion*; and that, as such, it may be *partial* — it may contain *bias*, and be based on stated or unstated *values*.

General Studies is about issues. You need to ask about any issue:
- What are the *facts* in the case?
- Is the evidence in the case *hard* or *soft*?
- Are *opinions* expressed well supported by facts?
- Are opinions biased by *values* or *beliefs* held?

Marks will be given for AO4 when you show that you are not accepting statements at face value — just because they are in black and white. You will need to show awareness of the difference between facts and opinions; and between an objective statement and a subjective, partial judgement — one that may be biased by *values* that may be shared by many people, or by very few.

Here is an example of differences in the context of a particular General Studies issue — global warming, or climate change.
- It is an *objective fact* that the mean temperature of the biosphere has risen by approximately 0.5°C in the last 100 years.
- It is a *theory*, based on quite *hard evidence*, that greenhouse gases have contributed to this warming.
- The evidence gives rise to the *opinion* that we should act to reduce the emission of greenhouse gases.

- Climate change challenges the *value* that we attach to ownership and use of vehicles burning fossil fuels.
- There is a *belief* among 'greens' that we should cease to worship the god of economic growth.

Finally, it is important that you recognise that our knowledge about any issue — the causes of it, and the consequences of it — is likely to be limited. It is appropriate to be sceptical about claims to certain knowledge, or indisputable opinions. The advice is not to be perverse — but, in general, to prefer questions to answers.

Section 1
Document response

Section 1

Examiners in General Studies cannot ask you many questions on subjects that they know you have learnt. The specifications published by the boards do not list topics that you must know all about, learn almost by heart and revise. All they do is define areas within which questions might be set. Because these are likely to be quite broad, stimulus material may well be supplied on, or with, the examination paper. Questions of a quite sharply focused kind can then be asked on this material. Sometimes the material is pictorial or diagrammatic, but generally it is a paragraph or longer passage of prose.

In the general introduction to this book I made the claim that 'ultimately, knowledge is indivisible'. Unfortunately it is all too often divided, for convenience, into three blocks: (a) the arts, (b) the social sciences and (c) the (natural and physical) sciences.

These blocks are not made of granite; they are made of fast-melting ice. (Is cultural studies an arts subject or a social science? Is psychology a social science or a natural science?) The more we try to partition them, the faster they melt into each other. Still, for practical purposes I have adopted this conventional division of knowledge in this book.

In Section 1 there are four passages each on arts, social sciences and sciences. The third and fourth passages in each block are paired: they are on the same subject and afford opportunities for comparison and contrast. In each case I have set three different tasks, of a sort commonly set on present-day and forthcoming papers. These are as follows:
(a) **Multiple-choice questions:** usually five on the first passage, eight on the second, and ten — five each — on the paired passages.
(b) **Short-answer questions:** usually seven on the first passage and eight on subsequent passages. These are comprehension questions in the main. My own 'answers' to these run to two or three lines only — but each is capable of some expansion.
(c) **An essay:** the requirement after the first passage, in each of the three blocks, is for a 'short essay'. The 'answer' that I have supplied to this question, at the end of this section (pp. 11-12), is of between 300 and 400 words. I supply longer essay answers to the questions following the second, third and fourth passages in each block. These range in length from about 600 to 800 words. There is no optimum length for either a short or a long essay. The important thing is that you should say what you have to say clearly, in a logical order — and that you should come to a conclusion that answers the question.

I shall have more to say about writing essays in my introduction to Section 3 of this book. Here it is enough to outline the principles on which I base the essays that you will find throughout the book.
(a) **The introduction:** this has two functions, i.e. to make clear (i) the meaning of the question or essay title and (ii) how you intend to answer the question, or address the title. (If the meaning of the question/title is perfectly clear already, then all you need by way of introduction is a statement of intent.)

Document response

(b) **The argument:** many (perhaps most) essays are debates between two positions.

> **Q** 'It is customary nowadays for students to take time out from study to go back-packing, for example, to India. Do you think it is better to do this before embarking on university studies, or afterwards?'
>
> or
>
> **Q** 'Is it more important, in your view, to engage in sport for one's health or for simple enjoyment?'

Much of any essay will be a setting out of the evidence, first for one position and then for the other. It is important to give examples in order to illustrate the positions, particularly in the context of the position that you support. I would suggest that you place this second, since it will then lead straight to your conclusion.

(c) **The conclusion:** this should follow straight from the argument, and be based on it. It will already have become clear where the argument is headed: there is no need for you to pretend that you remain open-minded until the very last line. Indeed, you might already have declared your hand in your statement of intent. You need not come down on one side or the other if you genuinely think the question remains open — but in this case you might suggest what further evidence would be necessary to help you to make up your mind.

When an essay doesn't naturally fall into two contrasting or complementary positions it probably lends itself to an argument that consists of a sequence of points, or a list. Most of the 'answers' that I have provided for the essay questions in this section are two-position essays. You are more likely to be asked 'Why' questions — or 'To what extent...' or 'How far ...' questions — than simple 'What' questions.

Finally, this is probably the best place to explain how and why the essays (as well as all other answers to questions in this book) came to be written. I did not have very long in which to put this Question and Answer Guide together — and you will not have very long in which to write your answers to the questions on the examination papers. For both of these reasons I tried not to let my pen run away with me:

- I tried (and, in the main, succeeded in) writing each of the essays at one sitting.
- I did not have source material to hand as I wrote the essays — each was written 'off the top of my head'.
- I did not revise the essays once they were finished.

Had I written the essays in the manner in which I generally prepare material for publication, the result might have looked altogether beyond what it would be possible to achieve in examination conditions. I sought to avoid this, and in consequence ran the risk of giving an unpolished performance. Perhaps it will not be the least useful aspect of this book that I leave myself wide open to your considered criticism and suggestions for improvement.

Section 1 Arts

What is art?

Call this art?

A lot of people said a lot of rude things about the paintings of Picasso, Braque, Matisse, Léger and other abstract artists painting before and after the First World War. Their work appeared to lack skill and it was often difficult to guess what a painting was intended to represent. A title sometimes helped; sometimes it added to the problem.

The problem grew bigger in America (where most things grow bigger) after 1945. Jackson Pollock did not paint on an easel: he laid the canvas flat on the floor. He squeezed paint onto it straight from the tube; he flicked and threw paint onto it; he used his fingers and his feet to make patterns in it; he even rode a bicycle over it. When members of the public saw such paintings they said: 'I could have done that' or 'A 4-year-old could have done that' or 'A chimpanzee could have done that — and made a better job of it too'. Paintings ceased to be pictures. The paintings of Mondrian, Kandinsky and Klee were no longer paintings of anything: they seemed more like wallpaper designs. People still asked questions about what they saw ('Is it art?', 'What's it about?', 'What's it supposed to represent?') but they no longer expected intelligible answers. The public regarded modern art, like 'serious' music and free verse, as a province beyond its understanding.

This did not prevent the public being critical, however. When London's Tate Gallery paid several thousand pounds for Carl André's *Equivalent 8*, people were not sure whether to be amused or scandalised. André's 'sculpture' consists of two layers of 60 ochre firebricks, one laid neatly on top of the other. People say of it: 'I could have done it', 'A 4-year-old could have done it', 'Did the builders leave them behind?' Whatever else might be said about these, no chimpanzee could have laid the bricks in such a straight line!

The people who guard 'the Bricks' and other works of modern art hear all these comments several times daily. Robert Ryman, a guard at the Museum of Modern Art in New York, decided that he probably *could* do better himself. He is an 'abstract expressionist', like Pollock. He paints whole canvases with white paint, though sometimes oranges and greens peep out from under the white. Art critics said of André's 'Bricks' that they 'represent order in a disordered world'. Of Ryman's mostly white paintings they say that they 'draw attention to the importance of light in painting', that they are about 'physical sensation', even that they are 'paintings about painting'. Critics have to be almost as creative as the artists themselves where much modern art is concerned — indeed, they are perhaps more creative than Robert Ryman. Whilst the director of the Tate Gallery praises the artists for having 'stretched the boundaries of painting', Ryman himself denies that there is any meaning in his all-white canvases. 'They're paintings,' he says, 'not pictures.' Ryman giggles when he hears critics talk about his work. The artist is almost as childlike in his simplicity as his paintings.

Even he is not as childlike, however, as Carly Johnson. If visitors to Manchester City Art Gallery had stood in front of her *Rhythm of the Trees* and said a 4-year-old could have done it, they would have been right: Carly Johnson is just 4 years old. Mrs Johnson, Carly's mother, had heard so many silly things said by so many silly critics about so many silly paintings that she thought she would enter Carly's painting for the Manchester Academy of Fine Arts annual show, for a joke. More than 1,100 paintings were entered for this competition and only 150 were accepted. Young Carly's *Rhythm of the Trees* was one of them. The judges liked it for its 'quality of colour balance, composition and technical skill'. Carly herself said: 'It's just a little pattern'. It was Carly's mother who had thought up the title; to Carly, the 'trees' were no more than shapeless blobs.

Six visitors to Manchester City Art Gallery liked Carly's painting enough to want to buy it, even at Mrs Johnson's 'joke' of an asking price: £295. The Irish art collector who bought it said it was a 'gorgeous' picture. Mrs Johnson was asked what Carly would do with the money. 'I don't know,' she said, 'but I think she's fed up with painting so she probably won't want to buy paints.'

Carly could perhaps do worse with her money than buy a good big pile of firebricks. It would be a daily reminder to her of the strange, disordered world we live in.

Multiple-choice questions

1 Why were people rude about the paintings of Picasso and others?
 A Their work lacked skill.
 B The titles they chose were often confusing.
 C They seemed not to represent anything.
 D The paintings were crude and artless.

2 The public no longer expected to understand modern art because:
 A It was as unintelligible as much music and poetry.
 B Abstract paintings seemed to break all the old rules about what 'art' is.
 C A 4-year-old could have painted the works of Jackson Pollock.
 D Artists were enjoying themselves at the expense of an ignorant public.

3 Critics are said to be as 'creative' as the artists themselves, in that:
 A They are able to see the hidden meanings in paintings.
 B They have a hard job helping the public to understand modern art.
 C Critics have to create pictures out of mere paintings.
 D They have had to use criteria of judgement as modern as the art itself.

Section 1

4 Manchester City Art Gallery chose Carly's painting because:
  A It seemed to possess the qualities of good abstract art.
  B It really was painted by a 4-year-old.
  C It was clearly a painting that would command a good price.
  D It was a lot more interesting than a white canvas or a line of bricks.

5 An Irish art collector bought the painting because:
  A It appears he liked it for its own sake.
  B He thought it remarkable for a 4-year-old.
  C He appreciated Mrs Johnson's 'joke' of a price.
  D He respected the art gallery's judgement in choosing it.

Short-answer questions

6 What do you take the word 'abstract' to mean in the term 'abstract art'?

7 What seems to have been the 'problem' (l. 5) where much abstract art was concerned?

8 Why might the public have been 'amused' when the Tate Gallery bought *Equivalent 8*?

9 Why, instead of being amused, might they have been 'scandalised'?

10 What might the director of the Tate have meant when he said that Ryman had 'stretched the boundaries of painting'?

11 In what sense did Mrs Johnson herself think of her asking price for Carly's painting as a 'joke'?

12 Why might the Irish art collector nevertheless have been pleased to pay the asking price?

Short-essay question

What do you understand, from this article and elsewhere, to be the role of the art critic and of art criticism?

Answers

1 **(c)** You might agree with all the other possible answers but the passage only explicitly supports (c).

2 **(b)** This is the only 'factual' answer of the four.

3 **(d)** It may not be the critics' intention to help the public to understand art — and are we confident of their ability to see hidden meanings?

Document response

4 **(a)** (d) is undoubtedly true, but it would be speculative to suppose this was the gallery's reason.

5 **(a)** He called it 'gorgeous'. The other answers may be true, but we cannot know for sure.

6 The word 'abstract' means (in this context) non-representational. An abstract painting does not represent nature; it is abstracted from it.

7 The 'problem' seems to have been that paintings, rather suddenly, had no obvious meanings or referents. They were not 'of' anything or 'about' anything.

8 The public might have been 'amused' because it might have thought that the Tate was behaving true to form. The public might have had its suspicions as to the fatuousness of much 'modern art' confirmed.

9 The public might have been 'scandalised' by the waste of public money on a 'silly' piece of work.

10 He might have meant that Ryman had redefined painting; he had identified one more artistic possibility; he had refused to be bound by convention.

11 Mrs Johnson probably thought that it was an outrageous price for a child's 'pattern'. The joke was on the whole silly, sententious art establishment.

12 He might have been pleased because he liked the painting so enormously; and because its brief notoriety might have increased its value in the long term.

Short-essay question

Whilst there is no obvious conflict between two positions here, you could argue that on the one hand the critic is an intermediary between artist and public, with a (self-imposed?) role to 'explain' the former to the latter (Position A); yet on the other hand most critics seem to want to keep the public at bay, or to be addressing only a small highbrow section of it — even, perhaps, to be the intermediaries between artists and art dealers (Position B). This is how I shall argue here.

Critics are generally employed by a newspaper or magazine to review an exhibition of an artist's work. A major new exhibition, or a retrospective collection, of an artist's works is news: so there is every justification for an article about it. Since much art does not speak for itself it makes sense for the reviewer to be something of an 'expert' in art history, iconography or cultural studies. A critic is a judge (this is what the word means), and a good judge bases his or her judgement on knowledge and understanding. A good critic passes on some of this knowledge and understanding to the gallery-going public. Lord Clark was such a critic: he was able in his television series (and accompanying book), *Civilisation*, to supply a background for the paintings he commented upon, and therefore to enhance our understanding of where the artists were 'coming from'.

> Too often, however, critics seem to want to follow fashion rather than to interpret it — never mind lead it. It is fashionable to be avant-garde (it was for most of the twentieth century). It was 'cool' to say of André's 'Bricks' (*Equivalent 8*) that they 'represent order in a disordered world'; it would not have been cool to say that they were an expensive spoof. It is as if the public was 'wrong', in some objective sense, to say that they were just bricks, and the critics had to put them right. We expect critics to tell us something about Jackson Pollock's motive for splashing paint on his canvases; we even expect them to have opinions, and to express them — but do we need them to tell us what to think?
>
> It seems, sometimes, in their advocacy of modern art, that critics have an investment in our taking it seriously, as if their livelihood depended on the artists' livelihood and reputation. Critics with vested interests do not make good judges.
>
> *(318 words)*

A04 I have suggested that there is some *knowledge* about art that a good critic passes on. I cast doubt on whether it is possible to be *objective* about any particular work of art. A critic's judgement can probably be no more than a well-based *opinion*. This opinion may not, indeed, be *impartial*: what is good for the art business is good for art-criticism.

Section 1 Arts

Media violence

Media violence and children revisited: return to the killing screens?

From 'penny dreadfuls' to the recent downloading of pornography from the Internet, each new form of media technology has brought in its wake a new wave of public anxiety over media effects on impressionable members of society. Screen violence and its supposed effects on the audience has yet again appeared on the political agenda: Conenberg's film *Crash* has raised considerable public anxiety over questions of taste and the possibility of 'copycat' incidents. The controversy led to the temporary banning of the film by Westminster Council.

This concern about the potentially harmful effects of media violence on young audiences has united the political left and right. The effects debate was clearly articulated in the well-publicised case of the murder of the toddler James Bulger in 1993 by two young boys. The judge in summing up said, 'I suspect that exposure to violent video films may in part be an explanation' (*The Guardian*, 26 November 1993). The subsequent parliamentary call for action was clear evidence of a moral panic about the effects of screen violence on children.

In 1994, there were political moves to introduce new laws to reduce the availability of violent videos to young people. In the USA, in 1996, the V-chip was introduced, which would allow parents to censor the programmes available on television. Screen violence still feeds fears about deleterious media effects and also contributes to the easy scapegoating of the media for the general social malaise.

Clearly, children do imitate what they see on the screen, from the actions of *Power Rangers* to the pro-social activities of *Blue Peter*. However, concern has been expressed over the more serious forms of screen violence. Recent instances of 'copycat' violence in the nineties, including the supposed influence of the film *Natural Born Killers* on 16-year-old Nathan Martinez (who murdered his stepmother and half-sister after seeing the film ten times) and the alleged connection between James Bulger's murder and *Child's Play 3*, led to the commissioning by the British Board of Film Classification of another study into the viewing habits of young offenders by the Policy Studies Institute (PSI).

The results of this study showed no evidence that juvenile delinquents were exposed to or chose to watch more screened violence than their 'conformist' counterparts. The researchers concluded that 'considerable doubt can be cast upon claims of some direct causal connection or correlation between television and anti-social behaviour'. Significantly, they argued that: 'The overriding impression gained from interviewing [the offenders] was of lives that were full of change,

Section 1

chaos and deprivation, in which the media were of less significance than was the case for the non-offending peers'.

By contrast, Professor Elizabeth Newson's discussion paper, 'Video violence and the protection of children', lent support to a New Right campaign launched in 1993 to protect children from the supposedly harmful effects of video nasties. She claimed that 'professionals in child health and psychology under-estimated the degree of brutality and sustained sadism that film-makers were capable of inventing'. She argued that studies proved an effect between violence on screen and real-life aggression in children and teenagers.

However, Scandinavian research showed: 'Mass communication research has not been able to discern any corresponding causal relation between entertainment violence and violent crimes.' Instead, 'different persons experience excitement, violence, horror and power — as well as other media and cultural contexts — very differently, need it differently and attach different meanings to it' (von Feilitzen 1994). Still, researchers continue to hold competing interpretations on the relationship between television and violence.

Source: 'Media violence and children revisited: return to the killing screens?', by Marsha Jones, SOCIOLOGY REVIEW, Vol.7, No.1, September 1997.

Multiple-choice questions

1 What were 'penny dreadfuls'?
  A   Black-and-white 'action' comics costing one penny.
  B   Penny-in-the slot, silent 'thriller' films.
  C   Blue movies that it cost a penny to watch, in the 1920s.
  D   Slot-machine, 'what-the-butler-saw' lantern slides.

2 What meaning does the word 'supposed' (l. 4) lend to the point the writer is making?
  A   The effects of screen violence can only be guessed at.
  B   The copycat effects of watching TV violence are well supported.
  C   There are alleged effects, but there is no hard evidence for them.
  D   The so-called effects are no more than prejudiced opinion.

3 What do you understand the writer means by a 'moral panic', in lines 13–14?
  A   A tendency to moralise, on the part of politicians.
  B   An anxiety in Parliament about the moral health of the nation.
  C   Politically motivated fear-mongering by MPs.
  D   Public fear of child murder, exploited by callous politicians.

4 '... the easy scapegoating of the media for the general social malaise.' What might this mean?

Document response

   A The media are hypocritical in pointing the finger at society at large.
   B Society is morally sick, and the media merely reflect this sickness.
   C A morally anxious public is too susceptible to media influence.
   D It is altogether too simple to blame the media for society's ills.

5 The Policy Studies Institute research showed that:
   A There is little evidence for a one-to-one relationship between watching screen violence and engaging in offending behaviour.
   B Young offenders appear to be particularly drawn to screen violence and to subsequent copycat behaviour.
   C There is no relationship whatsoever between the amount of violence watched on screen and violence perpetrated in reality.
   D Antisocial behaviour is present already; watching TV violence merely reinforces it.

6 The researchers concluded that:
   A If anything, screen violence has a worse effect on non-offenders.
   B Screen violence is of less significance than other violence in offenders' lives.
   C Offenders watch much less television than had been supposed.
   D There is much more that is disturbing in offenders' lives than TV violence.

7 The 1993 'video nasties' campaign was launched by:
   A Professionals in child health and psychology.
   B Religiously inclined Conservative politicians.
   C Conservatives opposed to all that Mrs Thatcher had stood for.
   D Libertarians arguing for a return to the 'permissive society'.

8 A 'causal relationship' between entertainment violence and violent crimes would imply that:
   A There is a loose, or casual, relationship between watching and doing.
   B Violence in society is what leads to much violence on screen.
   C Violent behaviour is a direct product of watching screen violence.
   D Screen violence has nothing to do with what happens in reality.

Short-answer questions

9 Who might be considered to be the 'impressionable members of society' (l. 3)?

10 'Public anxiety over questions of taste' (ll. 5–6): what is meant by 'taste' in this context?

11 What did the V-chip (l. 16) give parents that they had not had before?

12 In what sense might the activities of *Blue Peter* be called 'pro-social'?

13 Why do you suppose the word 'conformist' (l. 30) is placed in inverted commas?

Section 1

14 Why might media violence play a more significant — or influential — part in the lives of non-offenders than in the lives of offenders?

15 Should film-makers be encouraged by the findings of von Feilitzen, in Scandinavia?

Essay question

Make the case **either** for **or** against systematic censorship of screen violence on our television screens.

Answers

1 (a) They were comics featuring larger-than-life characters, of which adults, by convention, disapproved.

2 (c) Some people suppose there to be harmful effects, but evidence for these effects is, so far, unforthcoming.

3 (b) MPs voiced anxieties about a 'moral vacuum' in the nation, and searched about for simple causes and culprits. (They might have moralised as well — answer (a) — but the passage does not tell us this.)

4 (d) The media offered themselves as an easy target for politicians' accusations of moral laxity. The sins of a community were heaped on a 'scapegoat', in biblical times. (The word has only rather recently been used as a verb.)

5 (a) The alleged connection between watching screen violence and engaging in offending behaviour simply could not be shown. (Answer (c) is too strong — the complete absence of connection has not been shown either; and there is simply no warrant for answer (d).)

6 (d) 'Change, chaos and deprivation' are more disturbing for children than TV violence. (Answer (b) only refers to other 'violence' in offenders' lives.) To children who live otherwise undisturbed lives, TV violence may be the more disturbing.

7 (b) Religiously inclined (though not necessarily explicitly religious, still less fundamentalist) right-wing Conservatives — economic liberals, but moral absolutists.

8 (c) This is what the 'New Right' chose to believe; so far the cause–effect relationship has not been demonstrated.

9 Children are usually thought of as most 'impressionable' — but when does childhood end? Some people continue to be susceptible to all sorts of influences long after they have ceased to be children.

10 'Taste' in this context has to do with whether a programme would be considered vulgar or offensive, or fitting and acceptable, to a cross-section of mature members of the public.

Document response

11 It gave them the power to censor what their children watched. They had always been able simply to turn off the television; now their children were unable to subvert parents' intentions.

12 *Blue Peter* is a programme well known for its public-spiritedness, its positive images of society and its promotion of social betterment.

13 The writer may feel that 'conformist' is not quite the word that she wants; non-delinquents may not conform in other ways (conform to what model of a young person?) than by breaking the law.

14 Media violence might be the more shocking to well-adjusted youngsters than to the 'disturbed', because it offers more of a challenge to the life with which they are familiar.

15 The simple cause–effect relationship has been repudiated — but this only means that the relationship is hugely more complex. Film-makers still have responsibilities.

Essay question

The 'New Right' view may no longer be fashionable, and I do not personally subscribe to it — besides, 'censorship' has a whiff of the authoritarian about it. I shall nevertheless argue for censorship here, re-defining the word as I do so. It will be evident how my argument can be reversed.

I shall briefly refer to the A position, i.e. the dislike of censorship. Then I shall move to the B position, i.e. the need for restraint where screen violence is concerned:

Position A
Censorship is heavyhanded and illiberal.

Position B
Some (self-)restraint is, however, vital.

It is unlikely, perhaps, that your own answer would be as long as the following; but you would be expected to give some specific examples, as I do.

I shall discuss what might be meant by 'systematic' censorship (the 9.00 p.m. watershed; keeping the worst horror off-screen; the non-involvement of children; the refusal of 'gratuitous' violence) — and so conclude that controls are necessary if we are to call ourselves civilised.

We associate censorship with older-generation authoritarianism. It makes us think of moralising clergymen, schoolmasters, withered spinsters, and US Republicans and other 'conviction politicians'. The case for censorship is all too often made by those who will not admit to any moral uncertainty.

But at the other end of the continuum is the moral anarchist for whom 'anything goes'. Is that where any of us would comfortably stand? Could we really accept a situation in which killings, mutilation, sadism, ritual torture (to say nothing of pornography and sexual perversion) and other forms of violence were served up on our television screens — in our living rooms — without any controls being exercised whatsoever? To be sure, we could leave the television on stand-by, or heed warnings and turn it off. But in the first place, would we want to have to pursue avoidance measures more or less continuously; and in the second, would we be happy in the thought that other people might be indulging a taste for violence at second hand?

We have to accept that no correlation has been established between watching television violence and engaging in violent acts in reality — but this probably means that there is a complex rather than simple relationship between what we are exposed to and what we enact. It does not mean that there is no relationship at all. It has, therefore, to be assumed that some violence on television will have some unfortunate influence on some viewers. We shall probably want to protect some people (notably children) all of the time. Thus, we have PG, 15 and 18-rated films. We have a 9.00 p.m. watershed on television, and require that violent programmes are shown after this time, in the hope that all young children will be in bed. Even news programmes may have to be pruned of violent scenes if they are shown before this time.

Where there has to be some violence (for instance, in the screening of Dickens' *Oliver Twist* on children's television), the worst of it (in this case, the brutal murder of Nancy by Bill Sykes) should not be shown on screen. Nor should children's fantasies be fed by seeing other children subjected to violence on screen. Arguably, adults (some of them not very mature adults, some of them child abusers and paedophiles) should not be presented with (and perhaps gratified by) such images either.

Sometimes we shall want to spare all people, all the time, the worst excesses of screen violence. *A Clockwork Orange*, by Anthony Burgess, is a violent novel; but few people have read it, relatively speaking — and they probably did not read it for its violence. Stanley Kubrick, who made a film of the novel, soon came to realise that some people would watch the film for its violence — so he withdrew it from public viewing, as it was his right to do. If the best sort of censorship (or restraint) would have been not to make the film in the first place, Kubrick's was the second-best sort of censorship: self-censorship (or self-restraint). The violence in the novel is gratuitous — that is the point; but the reader 'sees' it only in the imagination. Gratuitous (or random and motiveless) violence on screen is potentially much more disturbing.

Self-restraint is a mark not of a censorious, but of a civilised society. To oppose 'censorship', and to impose every gory detail of a violent act upon an audience, is to be just as morally absolutist, just as certain, just as illiberal, as to want to return to the bad old days of the watch committee and the Lord Chamberlain's blue pencil. There has to be restraint, and it has to be systematic if it is not to be arbitrary. Acceptable standards will range up and down the continuum — but we should not allow ourselves to be pushed to either of the extreme ends.

(694 words)

A04 The point is made that — particularly in the absence of *hard evidence* for a positive relationship between TV-watching and violent behaviour — there is little or no room in this debate for *certainty*. If censorship is a matter of *opinion*, we need not agree with opinion at either extreme.

Section 1 Arts

The literary canon

Passage 1: The canon

The words 'canon' and 'canonical' (meaning belonging to the canon) are terms borrowed by literary criticism from the early Christian church. In church usage the canon means the books of the Bible, that have been accepted by the Church as being inspired by God.

In literary-critical usage the word canon means, roughly speaking, 'those books and authors that are accepted as belonging to English literature' (or French or German or Hungarian literature, if those are the canons under discussion, or the whole of Western literature, if that is the subject of debate).

In church usage what belongs to the canon can immediately be identified. It is the books of the Bible. In literary usage this is not so. There are some authors whom most people, if asked, would nominate as belonging to the canon of English literature — Shakespeare, Milton and Wordsworth, for example. But is Henry Constable (1562–1613) canonical, or Ambrose Philips (1674–1749), or Mrs Humphry Ward (1851–1920)? These writers, with hundreds of others, are listed in *The Oxford Companion to English Literature*. Obviously the question is unanswerable, since the literary canon is not a definite entity as the biblical canon is. It follows that much argument about the canon is equivalent to chasing shadows.

Those who rank themselves as opponents of what they perceive as the literary canon include feminists, gays, lesbians and Afrocentrists. They argue that the canon is imposed by the dominant institutions of the Western world as an instrument of sexist and racist oppression. To be forced to accept that literature is something written by dead white European males (DWEMs), and to be obliged to read this in order to qualify as educated, represents, these activists protest, a tyrannical conformity. Accordingly, they believe the canon should be changed to accommodate a wide range of writers representing different cultural, racial and sexual categories.

The usual reply, made by those who regard themselves as defenders of the canon, is that literary canons are not invented by institutions, but are determined by the gradually accumulating approval of readers, as well as by writers, who identify the authors of the past they can learn from.

Another argument used by canon-defenders is that English writers generally reckoned canonical include many, such as Bunyan, Swift, Dickens and Orwell, who were fiercely critical of institutions of authority. Indeed, viewed politically, the literary canon (these defenders argue) comprises an extraordinary bunch of loners, rebels and misfits. Hence the charge that the canon has been imposed

Section 1

by the governing institutions looks unlikely, since no institution anxious to impose its authority would choose such writers as its representatives.

Canon-defenders also back up their case by remarking that when the canon has changed in the past it has not been the result of any institutional decree, but has simply followed the changing taste of readers. John Donne and Andrew Marvell, they observe, have come into the canon in the twentieth century. Abraham Cowley (1618–67) has gone out (though in his day he was reckoned a major poet). It would be impossible to trace this change to a conspiracy of governments or institutions. Rather it reflects spontaneous processes of cultural change, not ascribable to any single source.

Protests against the literary canon began in the United States in the 1960s, and were part of the upheaval in American schools and universities sparked by opposition to the United States' role in the Vietnam War. This coincided with a fall-off in reading habits and an upsurge of television-viewing among the young, which gave impetus to the rejection of the often lengthy works of the traditional 'great authors'. Critical theory, women's studies, black writing and other alternatives gained recruits accordingly.

There seems now to be a backlash against these tendencies. The voice of America's new conservatism, as it applies to literary and educational issues, was resoundingly heard in Allan Bloom's best seller, *The Closing of the American Mind* (1987), which attacked multiculturalism, the abandonment of the 'great books' of the Western tradition, and the craven dismantling of American university education by supine, 'liberal' professors. More recently, Germaine Greer, in *Slip-Shod Sibyls: Recognition, Rejection and the Woman Poet* (1995), has questioned the value of many of the women authors who were 'rediscovered' in order to fill the syllabuses of the new women's writing courses.

If, as defenders of the canon have often claimed, it enshrines intrinsic literary value, then its defence is presumably unnecessary since its intrinsic value will ensure its survival.

Source: 'The canon', by John Carey, THE ENGLISH REVIEW, Vol. 7, Issue 1, September 1996.

Passage 2: To be outstanding

The writer who sends a mould-breaking novel to a publisher must expect to be told: 'This would be a difficult novel to sell because it does not fit into any of the usual categories.' There is an established readership for the western; there is another for the historical romance; and there is another still for the spy thriller. Yet westerns, historical romances and spy thrillers are not often called 'literature'. They sell in dependable numbers and for this reason publishers happily invest money in their publication, confident of a return on their investment.

Document response

Such novels as these have a short life, however; and they will not be reviewed, as a rule, on the arts pages of quality newspapers. The novels to which reviewers pay most attention are so-called 'novels of ideas', or 'literary' novels. They do not fit into any of the usual categories, and therefore publishers are unwilling to invest in them. An 'original' novel is a bad risk because it has no certain market. Yet it is the original novel that wins the Booker Prize, or the Guardian, or Goncourt, or other prestige award. It is never the fast-selling crime novel, or the pink-clad romance.

A novel, a play, a poem might stand out from the crowd — it might, that is, be outstanding or be perceived to be outstanding for any one of a number of reasons. E.M. Forster's early novels are works of consummate craftsmanship, but they cannot really be said to have broken new ground. *Maurice* was a different matter altogether. This was a fictional expression of his own homosexuality. It would have been explosive to publish it at the time of its writing, therefore Forster instructed that it be published only after his death. His wish was granted, and *Maurice* was duly published in 1971, by which time — such was the social and legal change that had taken place — the novel had lost much of its power to shock. Homosexuality is now a theme embedded in the modern novel as firmly as espionage, so that it can feature in a first novel — such as Peter Ackroyd's *The Great Fire of London*, of 1982 — and be as unremarkable as plain sin.

The non-conforming novel or play advertises its non-conformity perhaps most shockingly in its affront to the 'public morals' of its day. *Maurice* would have been such an affront if it had been published 20 years earlier.

James Joyce's *Ulysses* (its brothel scenes and its sexual fantasising) and D.H. Lawrence's *Lady Chatterley's Lover* (with its explicitness and rough-tongued, honest sexual language) tested even the newly emancipated temper of the early 1920s: *Ulysses* had to be smuggled into Britain from Paris; and *Lady Chatterley's Lover* had to wait until 1961 before all the spice was put back into it that had been taken out before.

The 'new morality' of the early 1960s made it possible for novelists and playwrights to explore themes that had lain dormant for generations. Not since the Restoration period (the late 1600s) in England had sex been so paraded. Shelagh Delaney's play *A Taste of Honey*, of 1958, highlighted juvenile love (and lovemaking); Lynne Reid Banks's *The L-Shaped Room* and Stan Barstow's *Saturday Night and Sunday Morning* raised the blinds on lusty non-conforming lives. These were the years of the Pill, and — in consequence — of casual sex and soon-made, soon-unmade relationships. To conform was for the girl to keep herself for 'Mr Right', and to walk to the altar with him as chaste as the day she was born; to be non-conformist was to be promiscuous, and to be impatient of 'Victorian' constraints. A novel or play, therefore, to be non-conformist, had to outdo its predecessors in the number of its bedroom scenes and in the directness of its language. It would not be long before nudity was brought to the stage, and simulated sex, heterosexual and homosexual alike.

Novelists and playwrights have not yet exhausted sex, or been exhausted by it — but they have to seek other themes in order to be 'original'. One such was social class: the 1944 Education Act opened up the grammar schools to working-class pupils of merit; post-war Britain was to be a 'meritocracy', and all would have an equal chance to climb the ladder of opportunity. It did not quite turn out like this. There were children from humble origins who went on to provincial universities (themselves featured in novels like Kingsley Amis's *Lucky Jim*, 1954, Malcolm Bradbury's *Eating People is Wrong*, 1959, and *The History Man*, 1975); but men — and it was still mostly men — from independent schools, who went on to Oxford or Cambridge, continued to secure the really top-class jobs. It was this injustice that Jimmy Porter was angry about in *Look Back in Anger* (1956), and that the upper-class Pip fought against in Arnold Wesker's *Chips with Everything* (1962). To be an angry young man in the late 1950s/early 1960s was to be non-conformist and outstanding — but neither anger, nor originality, is easily sustained.

Violence was another taboo that had to be broken sooner or later. Edward Bond fell foul of the Lord Chamberlain with his stage-play *Saved* (1965), in which a baby is stoned in its pram; and his *Lear*, of 1971, is a re-working of the Shakespeare tragedy that exploits all the elements of physical violence in the play to the full.

The 'greatest' novels and plays of the twentieth century are precisely those works that do not fit into any category; they are the works of observant commentators at least, of prophets at best. Each of them is a 'one-off', without obvious precedent, and without successful imitator. The real non-conformists are the artists: John Steinbeck was one, when he wrote *The Grapes of Wrath*; V.S. Naipaul was another, when he wrote *The House of Mr Biswas*; and Primo Levi was a third, when he wrote *The Periodic Table*. Among playwrights, Samuel Beckett will earn his place for *Waiting for Godot* and Brecht for *The Caucasian Chalk Circle*. We will have our own list of those works that 'stand out in our minds'. They were all, as likely as not, works that publishers rejected.

Multiple-choice questions

Passage 1: The canon

1 What do we mean by 'the canon of English literature'?
   A   The books contained in the English Bible.
   B   Works studied in university English literature departments.
   C   All the works listed in *The Oxford Companion to English Literature*.
   D   Works having literary value that stand the tests of time and public taste.

2 Argument about the canon is 'equivalent to chasing shadows' in that:
   A   There is no fixed canon of literary works as there is of biblical books.
   B   Most of the writers whose works are included are dead.

Document response

C   Much of the literature of the past is out of print and therefore unavailable.
D   There are hundreds of contenders, so no one can have read them all.

3 Why do minority groups object to the whole notion of a 'canon'?
   A   They resent their favourite authors being excluded.
   B   They support a *laissez-faire* attitude towards what literature is.
   C   'The canon' has been chosen by dominant social–cultural groups.
   D   The canon seems to include a strange bunch of misfits and loners.

4 Defenders of the canon assert that:
   (i)   Official institutions simply cannot have imposed the canon.
   (ii) Certain writers have entered, and left, the canon at different times.
   (iii) It is readers who choose what is canonical and what is not.
   (iv) Many writers are canonical whom no élite would have chosen.

   Answer:
   A   if (i) and (iv) only are correct.
   B   if (iii) only is correct.
   C   if all are correct.
   D   if (ii) and (iv) only are correct.

5 Bloom's and Greer's books were an attempt to:
   A   Discredit the whole notion of canonical works.
   B   Re-establish standards of critical judgement.
   C   Undermine the influence of the old literary establishment.
   D   Restore the reputation of long-forgotten authors.

Passage 2: To be outstanding

6 Publishers are wary of accepting 'mould-breaking' novels because:
   A   It is difficult to ensure that such novels will be reviewed.
   B   Such novels do not win any of the great literary prizes.
   C   Original novels are difficult to market successfully.
   D   They require more investment than westerns and romances.

7 *Maurice* is outstanding among Forster's novels in that:
   A   It was published much later than all the others.
   B   It dealt with a highly controversial subject.
   C   It is a work of consummate craftsmanship.
   D   It brought about a change in attitudes towards homosexuality.

8 Sexually non-conformist works had to:
   (i)   Be more daring than others to make themselves noticed.
   (ii) Wait, generally, until the 1960s to be published in full.
   (iii) Defy the conventions of the surviving 'Victorian' morality.
   (iv) Break with the 'new morality' of the early 1960s.

Answer:
A if (iv) only is correct.
B if (i), (ii) and (iii) are correct.
C if (i) and (iii) only are correct.
D if (i) only is correct.

9 A 'meritocracy' exists where:
   A All literary works have an equal chance of being published.
   B Anyone who shows promise can rise to the top in his or her field.
   C Middle-class males secure all the most lucrative jobs.
   D Children from humble origins go to provincial universities.

10 The works that appear to survive changing tastes are those that:
   A Have a dependable, 'niche' market.
   B Refuse to conform to the norms of the past.
   C Shocked the public at the time they were published.
   D Are works of art, standing on their own.

Short-answer questions (Passages 1 and 2)

11 Why do westerns, historical romances and spy thrillers not feature in the 'canon' of English literature?

12 How far do the books and authors referred to in Passage 2 justify the jibe in Passage 1 that 'literature' is written by dead white European males?

13 In what respect(s) do the two passages agree, where the power of 'governing institutions' (Passage 1) and 'the established order' (Passage 2) over the canon is concerned?

14 Passage 1 refers to 'spontaneous processes of cultural change'. What cultural changes does Passage 2 make mention of?

15 Do the passages agree or disagree about the impact of changes in the universities on what was accepted as 'English literature'?

16 What aspect of social non-conformity is referred to in Passage 1 that is absent from Passage 2?

17 What aspect of social non-conformity is referred to in Passage 2 that is absent from Passage 1?

18 Is the writer of Passage 1 likely to accept the Passage 2 reference to 'works that stand out in our minds' as a definition of 'the canon'?

Document response

Essay question

In an age in which the dominant media are visual, and more and more young people watch films and play computer games, how far does it matter that the younger generation may not develop the habit of reading novels?

Answers

1 **(d)** Works having literary value that survive changes in taste and social circumstances — works having intrinsic merit.

2 **(a)** There is nothing 'objective' about any critic's choice of 'great' works.

3 **(c)** They claim that the canon has been imposed on students from above.

4 **(c)** All are correct. Readers, not institutions, 'choose' what is canonical — though these readers may include publishers and film-makers.

5 **(b)** The standards of critical judgement needed to be re-established, after a period in which the 'canon' expanded (these writers allege) to include much mediocre work.

6 **(c)** It is risky to invest in them because they have no 'established readership'.

7 **(b)** Homosexuality was controversial when the novel was written; it was less controversial in 1971, when the novel was published.

8 **(b)** (i), (ii) and (iii) are correct. Such works were in tune with the 'new morality' of the 1960s.

9 **(b)** The deserving have the opportunity to succeed. The word was coined by Michael Young in his *The Rise of the Meritocracy*, of 1958.

10 **(d)** Almost nothing can be said about them as a separate class.

11 There is nothing new about them; they do not challenge conventional views; they have no intrinsic literary value, being written and published for purely financial reasons.

12 Shelagh Delaney and Lynne Reid Banks were not males; Barstow, Bradbury, Amis, Osborne and Wesker were not dead; and Steinbeck, Naipaul (Hemingway, Rushdie, etc. etc.) were not European.

13 They agree that the establishment has little or no power to determine what is in the canon and what is excluded. Both passages refer to a number of writers who rather confronted the establishment than conformed to it.

14 Growing acceptance of homosexuality, explicit sexuality, class mobility and violent scenes in novels and on stage are referred to.

15 They largely agree that as the universities grew, and as more working-class, female and ethnic-minority students studied there, so the notion of what was 'literary' expanded.

16 The issue of racism is largely absent from the account in Passage 2.

Section 1

17 Violence of a rather raw kind is not referred to in Passage 1. Perhaps violence had always been present in the literature of the USA, therefore its inclusion was not non-conformist or challenging.

18 It is likely that this definition would be acceptable to the writer of Passage 1. There is certainly no definition of the canon in Passage 1 that would contradict it.

Essay question

There are one or two sub-questions here that might be dealt with before the central question is addressed:
(a) Is it the case that the dominant media are visual?
(b) Are watching films/playing computer games and reading novels incompatible? Might not young people do all three things?

I shall answer these two questions before considering the two obvious positions, namely:

Position A	**Position B**
It doesn't matter that young people might not read novels.	It does matter that young people might not read novels.

> There can be no doubt about the importance of television as a medium of entertainment. The film — whether in broadcast or video-recorded form — is obviously a major constituent of many people's viewing, though the extent to which people watch television for information (for news and documentary programming) should not be underestimated. Fiction, therefore — or, more simply, the telling of stories — is a big part of young people's lives, even though it is in graphical rather than written form. The cinema has held its own against television in this respect; and in spite of developments in interactive video, and of the growing sophistication of computer games, the non-interactive fiction film is likely to continue to be a powerful medium of entertainment. This is not to say that the entertainment need be light. There was nothing 'low-brow' about Spielberg's *Schindler's List* — and Thomas Kenneally cannot have minded that millions of cinema-goers were made familiar with his hero's story who never would have read *Schindler's Ark*.
>
> Graphic media may be dominant, too, without the novel disappearing from the folk-memory and the culture. It is quite possible to watch films and play computer games and read novels — if not simultaneously. The serialisation on television of Jane Austen's *Pride and Prejudice* is well known for having stimulated many viewers to buy the novel and to read it for themselves — and their reading might well have profited from being fed by well-chosen, historically accurate visual images. Perhaps we have to face the fact that few young people (few people of any age) will readily embark on the reading of Dickens' *Great Expectations*, Eliot's *Middlemarch* or Fielding's *Tom Jones* nowadays, without the spur of a filmed version to bring an otherwise

Document response

increasingly alien experience a little closer. Nothing is being lost here, and much might be gained.

Many films, of course, and many film directors, depend on there being imaginative novels on which to base their films. Some of the most memorable films of recent years (*Howard's End, The Remains of the Day, The English Patient, Waterland*) depended upon there being memorable novels to base them on. Indeed, a well-made film may not only do justice to a novel: it may bring something extra to it. There may be many novels currently being written and published that would not suffer from being filmed. From the point of view of popular access to the ideas — or more often to the historical period or the events depicted — many quite ordinary novels might gain much from the interpretation placed upon them by thoughtful directors.

In other respects, however, there would be cultural loss from the passing of the novel-reading habit. (It might be wondered whether young people or indeed any generation, in the mass, have ever read novels out of habit. It has, perhaps, always been a minority pursuit. So we might ask ourselves if it would matter whether or not the younger generation — or a significant portion of the younger generation — ever acquired the habit.) It is not only film directors who would suffer the loss. Novels that achieve the status of 'literature' do so because there is more to them than a cinematic 'story'. Certain novels of ideas seem to defy filming. How would a director grapple with time running backwards as in Martin Amis's *Time's Arrow* without what is deeply serious in that marvellous novel being made laughable, even cartoon-like?

Perhaps we need not fear that the younger generation will cease to read worthwhile novels. Such novels will be written, published and read — as John Carey says — because they will be perceived to have 'intrinsic value'. To this extent, we can be optimistic that there will always be a 'market' for them. *(613 words)*

e The question bracketed above about whether young people have ever been in the habit of reading novels could alternatively have been included among the sub-questions raised at the beginning.

Time's Arrow is just a novel I happen to have read recently. You would need to be able to exploit whatever you might have had time to read — or rely on hearsay evidence. If you have not read any novels at all, your reference base is rather limited.

A04 As in painting, so in literature critical judgement is only a well-based *subjective opinion*. There is little room for *certain knowledge*. On the other hand, there is nothing trivial about *values* — the values on which criticism of a novel may be based go quite deep. They have to do with what we attach importance to in life.

Section 1 Social Sciences

Gender bias

Challenging gender biases

Feminist psychology is not just about proving that women are equal to men. Some feminist psychologists do accept that there may be ways in which females (on average) perform less well than males (in leadership abilities, or spatial and numerical skills, for example). Feminist psychologist Alice Eagly argues that the evidence does suggest that women show (on average) less leadership ability than do men. This does not mean, however, that women should not be allowed to be leaders — any more than the evidence showing that men are (on average) less good at verbal skills means that men should not be allowed to be writers. In the same way, if the evidence supports the view that women's spatial skills are inferior to men's, this does not mean that women should never be allowed to become architects or pilots.

Many feminist psychologists have also argued that differences between men and women have been over-emphasised. Eleanor Maccoby and Carol Jacklin, in 1974, surveyed all the existing psychological research on sex differences and concluded that for most areas of human functioning there was no evidence at all for differences between men and women, and that in those few areas where it did seem that differences existed, the differences were very small. In other words, there may be differences between men and women, but many of them are tiny, and there are other, much bigger, differences between people.

One of these much bigger differences is social role. It does not matter whether a person is a man or a woman — if you put them in specific social roles, they will behave in particular ways. Researchers have found that job applicants smile more than the person interviewing them for the job — whether the applicant is male or female and whether the interviewer is male or female. In another study, employed adults reported every day for 20 days on their interactions with their bosses and their co-workers. Submissive behaviours were self-reported more with bosses and less with co-workers — again, it did not make any difference what sex the person or the boss was. In other words, gender was not sufficient to explain smiling or submissive behaviour in these situations, but social role was.

Research on gender stereotypes suggests that people *believe* that differences between men and women are much bigger than they really are. This leads people to discriminate against women in some jobs (and, of course, against men in others) in ways that are unfair, because they do not reflect actual abilities.

Questions about sex similarities and sex differences are not just *scientific* questions — they are also highly *political*. In other words, the *science* of sex differences research is always used for *political* reasons — just as research on the differences between Black people and White people has always been used to defend

Document response

racist ideas, or to argue against them. However much psychologists may think or hope or believe that they are doing objective research and discovering truths about the world, they are always influenced (in ways they probably do not know about at the time) by the social and political context in which they are doing their research.

Source: 'Challenging gender biases', by Celia Kitzinger, PSYCHOLOGY REVIEW, Vol.4, No.3, February 1998.

Multiple-choice questions

1 The fact that women show, on average, less leadership ability than men means:
  A Some women will show more leadership ability than some men.
  B Women ought not to be encouraged to take up positions of leadership.
  C Most men are likely to be better leaders than all women.
  D On average, women are better at being led than men are.

2 Women architects and pilots:
  A Are likely to have inferior spatial skills in comparison with men.
  B Need more training than male architects and pilots.
  C Are likely to be fewer in number than male architects and pilots.
  D Have spatial skills that are superior to those of other women.

3 Differences between what men and women can do:
  A Have been grossly overstated by most psychologists.
  B Are not thought to be significant by feminist psychologists.
  C Are significant statistically, but not socially.
  D Are played down by feminist psychologists for political reasons.

4 The fact that job applicants smile more than job interviewers seems to indicate that:
  A Social role is more significant for behaviour than gender.
  B Female job applicants seek to charm male job interviewers.
  C Interviewing is even more stressful than being interviewed.
  D Job applicants are more confident in their social role than interviewers.

5 There is still discrimination against women because:
  A Feminist psychologists have not managed to get their message across.
  B People are over-impressed by the research evidence on gender differences.
  C Women are too submissive, and need to have assertiveness training.
  D Society at large thinks gender differences are bigger than they really are.

Short-answer questions

6 What do you understand by 'spatial skills' in the context of this passage?

Section 1

7 Does the evidence referred to in ll. 7–8 suggest that women writers are superior to their male counterparts?

8 Why do you suppose that functional differences between men and women have been over-emphasised in the past?

9 What did the research into submissive behaviour in the work-place indicate?

10 Why is discrimination said to be 'unfair'(l. 33)?

11 How is it said that the answers to questions about gender differences are used by those who ask the questions?

12 Why is it difficult — if not impossible — for researchers in social science to be 'objective'?

Short-essay question

'Discrimination, on any grounds whatsoever, is unjust and should not be tolerated in a free society.' Discuss.

Answers

1 (a) There is a very large gender overlap, so most women are as good at leadership as most men. Answer (d) is not implied, necessarily, by the premiss.

2 (c) They will be fewer in number simply because — on average — men are more likely to have the necessary skills.

3 (b) Answer (a) is too strong to be acceptable here.

4 (a) Applicants (male and female) smile more than interviewers because they perceive smiling as belonging to their role.

5 (d) People are unlikely to be aware of the research evidence, i.e. answer (b); they discriminate because this has been the norm.

6 They are the skills of judging distances, angles and other relationships between different objects in 2-D and 3-D space.

7 No. Averages say nothing whatsoever about individuals. Besides, 'verbal skills' is a rather vague term that may not capture what we mean by 'writing skills'.

8 It was a man's world, and it suited men to peddle the myth of their superiority. Besides, what was done had a powerful influence on what was thought should be done.

9 It indicated that a boss (male or female) is perceived as someone to whom it is proper to be submissive, whereas a co-worker is not. A boss occupies a socially superior role ex officio.

10 It is said to be unfair inasmuch as it is based on perceived rather than on real differences. It is based on stereotyping and prejudice.

Document response

11 The answers are used for 'political' purposes. That is, those who ask the questions make certain social-political presuppositions, and the answers tend to reinforce their preconditioned beliefs.

12 All social science research is conducted within a particular 'political' context — a context of power relationships. The researchers themselves are the products of this context, therefore they cannot be entirely neutral observers.

Short-essay question

What do we mean by discrimination? This question must be addressed first. A clear definition will help us to see that there are grounds for discrimination in certain circumstances.

Position A
Discrimination is advisable.

Position B
Discrimination is unjust.

The word 'discrimination' has acquired a rather unsavoury reputation in recent years, since it is the key word in legislation designed to promote fairness and equal opportunities. Discrimination in itself is perfectly respectable; indeed, to call an art collector or a wine taster 'discriminating' is a compliment. Someone who asks a particular person to marry them is being discriminating; a person who 'sleeps around' is not being discriminating: he or she is being promiscuous — or undiscriminating.

Even in the context of recruiting employees, it pays an employer to be discriminating. Of two candidates for the post of school bursar, the employer will choose the one who has the better grasp of budgeting processes. A security company that specifically wants a male bodyguard is legally entitled to discriminate in favour of male applicants. Likewise, a film director who is looking for a black female leading actress is legally permitted to discriminate against white women, women from the Far East, etc.

The important issue is whether the difference between two applicants for a job is relevant to the demands of that job. If a white library manager chooses a white applicant from a field of otherwise black applicants for a position as assistant librarian, he or she could not be accused of discrimination on racial grounds if the white applicant had come top in librarianship examinations. If the white applicant had come bottom, or was otherwise ill-suited to the position, then the manager might well have discriminated unjustly.

It must be our objective in a free society to eradicate unjust discrimination on racial, gender, religious and any other irrelevant grounds. But it will always be open to interpretation whether age, for example, is relevant or irrelevant in any particular circumstance — to say nothing of such emotive differences as obesity or physical handicap.

(300 words)

AO4 By being about *bias*, this is of its very nature an AO4 topic. Kitzinger had interesting things to say about what people *believe* about gender differences and the limits of *objectivity* in this research field.

Section 1 Social Sciences

Ethical foreign policy

New Labour, new ethics, new foreign policy?

In the postwar period academic debate on international relations has been dominated by the so-called 'realists', those who view the international system as a dangerous, highly unpredictable environment in which states exist in an atmosphere of hostility and mutual suspicion. Realists insist that within this 'anarchical society' foreign policy outcomes are determined by power politics, that is by the military, economic, and diplomatic resources which a state can mobilise behind its various demands. Given these underlying characteristics, a state should never allow the pursuit of its own interests to become entangled with wider moral or ethical considerations. Realists would dismiss these as, at best, a luxury and, at worst, a dangerous distraction from the 'real' political and economic world in which states must operate.

On 12 May 1997, less than a fortnight after assuming his reponsibilities, Robin Cook, the new Foreign Secretary in Britain's Labour government, entered this debate with a different message. In a speech delivered at the Foreign Office, Cook unveiled a set of proposals designed to put moral considerations generally and human rights in particular back 'at the heart of our foreign policy' (*Guardian*, 13 May 1997). The new Labour government's overseas strategy would have a strong 'ethical dimension' and it would not accept that 'political values can be left behind when we check in our passports to travel on diplomatic business'. The Conservative approach was now dismissed as outdated and — ironically, given its realist pretensions — unlikely to serve long-term British interests.

Here was the spectacle of a British Foreign Secretary standing the conventional logic on its head: British interests would be advanced not by a robust, and sometimes amoral, nationalism but by a more 'internationalist' policy, one which, in Cook's own words, 'supports the demands of other peoples for the democratic rights on which we insist for ourselves' (*Independent*, 13 May 1997). This approach seeks to make Britain a 'force for good in the world' by placing it at the head of a number of international campaigns with a distinct moral flavour.

By 1996 Britain had captured one quarter of the world defence market, becoming the world's second largest defence exporter behind the United States but ahead of France and Russia. The new government believes this brings with it a responsibility to ensure proper regulation of the arms trade. Britain will now press for a European Union-wide code of conduct, identifying regimes to whom the sale of arms should be prohibited for fear they will be used for internal repression or external aggression. In an early signal of intent Prime Minister Blair announced that Britain would implement a total ban on the manufacture and deployment of anti-personnel landmines and pledged to destroy all British stocks of these weapons by 2005. This was, he said, the 'right and the civilised thing to do'. The Foreign Secretary declared it to be evidence of Britain's determination to 'lead by force of example' (*Guardian*, 22 May 1997).

Profit will not be considered a dirty word but companies will be expected to recognise that their overseas operations cannot be based upon ruthless profiteering. This awareness needs to be reflected in the pay, conditions, and general treatment of their overseas workers. In particular, there is strong opposition to the use of child labour in the developing world, which is considered to be grossly exploitative and harmful to a child's educational and social development. Companies will also be encouraged to show greater awareness of the environmental impact of their activities.

The Foreign Secretary's 'mission statement' also suggested that Britain would seek to raise its profile in the area of international development. That position was further developed when Clare Short, the new Secretary of State for International Development, pledged a strong British role in the war on global poverty. This is a clear rejection of the previous administration's more *laissez-faire* approach. The Thatcher and Major governments confined themselves either to lecturing developing countries about the need for structural changes to their economies or to stressing that free trade and an expanding global economy will ultimately benefit all. Moreover, the aid budget was seriously reduced. When the Conservatives left office it had fallen to a mere 0.27% of Gross National Product (GNP), well short of the United Nations target figure of 0.7%.

Governments which respect human rights and practise democracy at home are believed to be more likely to uphold international law and with it their neighbours' rights and interests. Indeed, it has now become almost an iron law of international politics that democracies do not go to war with one another. The aim of policy, therefore, must be 'democratic enlargement' — to use the phrase of the Clinton administration — to make the world a more peaceful and orderly place. Conversely, dictatorships which repress their own citizens are held to be instinctively aggressive abroad. Saddam Hussein's Iraq provides only the most recent example of this. Appeasing such dictatorships only stores up future problems, as the experience with Saddam prior to the 1990–91 Gulf War demonstrates.

The defence industry employs, directly or indirectly, 360,000 people, and, in 1996, earned £5.1 billion for Britain in arms sales. Any government would think carefully before adopting policies which threatened to jeopardise this lucrative business. The government has also stressed that one of the key objectives of foreign policy is to boost British exports and jobs. Is this consistent with a moral approach to arms sales and an aversion to dictatorial regimes? The previous government encouraged the signing of huge arms contracts with Saudi Arabia (Britain's biggest customer) and Indonesia. Each of these has a very poor internal

Section 1

human rights record, and Indonesia also stands accused of aggression and genocide as a result of its 21-year occupation of East Timor. The new government may face strong pressure to end such deals but is it prepared to accept the negative impact on British trade and employment?

Faced with such complex issues, foreign policy may well become what it has traditionally been: an area of pragmatism, half measures and messy compromise. That would normally be acceptable, but Labour, with its evangelical tone and promise to introduce a new culture to foreign policy-making, has established more exacting standards by which it will now be judged.

Source: 'New Labour, new ethics, new foreign policy?', by James Hamill, POLITICS REVIEW, Vol.7, No.2, November 1997.

Multiple-choice questions

1 The 'realist' view of the world is of:
   A Two or three major powers trying to attain superpower status.
   B International anarchy where war is accepted as the norm.
   C Growing order imposed by a self-confident UN organisation.
   D States intent on serving their own best interests.

2 'Wider moral or ethical considerations' might be:
   A Issues of justice and equity, and democratic freedoms.
   B The pursuit of profit and competitive advantage.
   C Bringing international criminals to justice.
   D Curbing over-use of the world's natural resources.

3 By 'human rights' Cook might have meant:
   A Everybody's right to a European-style standard of living.
   B The right of every citizen to live in a democracy.
   C Freedom from want, and freedom to engage in the political process.
   D Equality of opportunity and outcome irrespective of status.

4 Britain's defence policy from May 1997 onwards would be to:
   A Lead the world in the sale of arms to responsible regimes.
   B Ban the sale of arms to Britain's major trade competitors.
   C Set an example by not selling arms to repressive governments.
   D Seek international agreement for constraints on arms sales.

5 What is meant by 'profiteering' (l. 43)?
   A Making profit by exploiting others and neglecting moral constraints.
   B Taking advantage of free trade to dump cheap goods on the market.
   C Seeking to make excessive profits by creating a monopoly.
   D Adopting a liberal economic policy where market forces rule.

Document response

6 The administrations of Thatcher and Major had not:
  A Attached much importance to expanding the global economy.
  B Concerned themselves with trying to meet the United Nations target.
  C Thought they could do anything to combat global poverty.
  D Done anything to promote market capitalism in poor countries.

7 The 'iron law' referred to in line 62:
  A Forbids war between democratic nations.
  B Is designed to make the world a more peaceful place.
  C Recognises that mature democracies do not fight each other.
  D Seeks to impose the 'American Way' on undemocratic states.

8 When states 'appease' a dictatorship, they:
  A Apply economic and political sanctions to it.
  B Overlook its moral failings to keep the peace.
  C Seek diplomatic means of doing business.
  D Lecture it on the need for sound ethical policies.

Short-answer questions

9 Why would 'realists' regard ethical considerations as a 'luxury'?

10 Why was it 'ironic' (l. 20) that Conservative policy was dismissed as out of date?

11 What would an 'internationalist' foreign policy look like as opposed to a 'nationalist' one?

12 What did the Foreign Secretary mean when he said Britain was 'determined to lead by force of example'?

13 How would British companies be expected to behave in their pursuit of profit overseas?

14 How might 'democratic enlargement' make the world a more peaceful and orderly place?

15 Why might Britain not want to make too much of 'ethical considerations' in dealings with regimes like Saudi Arabia?

16 What do you understand by 'pragmatism' in the context of the final paragraph?

Essay question

How far, in your view, should it be the business of the British government to concern itself with how other governments treat their citizens?

Section 1

Answers

1. **(d)** Answer (b) is too strong, and there is no warrant for (a) or (c) in the text. 'Realists' have little faith in international organisations.

2. **(a)** Cook refers to 'the demands of other peoples for the democratic rights on which we insist for ourselves'.

3. **(c)** Freedom to engage in the political process means freedom to vote, assemble, hold non-conformist views, etc. (sometimes referred to as 'civil rights'). Human rights are comprehensive, and start from the satisfaction of basic needs — for food and shelter as well as freedom.

4. **(d)** Britain did not want to be alone in banning exports to military regimes.

5. **(a)** Examples of exploitation include child labour, sweated labour and bonded labour. Profiteering has nothing to do with particular economic policies as in answers (b), (c) and (d).

6. **(b)** They had not made much attempt to raise the level of aid to 0.7% of the GNP. They did not believe that such 'untied' aid was economically very effective: it created 'dependency'.

7. **(c)** It is a descriptive, not a prescriptive law, as in (a).

8. **(b)** They overlook the failings to keep the peace — or in order to continue to do lucrative business, as Mrs Thatcher's government did with Saudi Arabia.

9. Britain could not afford to be too morally scrupulous in its trade relations with questionable regimes: (a) there are too many such regimes, and (b) we would lose out to our less squeamish competitors.

10. Conservative policy had put economic growth first and moral considerations second. Labour was now saying that a moral policy was a more effective economic — and security — policy.

11. An 'internationalist' foreign policy would take into account the shared values of the international community as well as (if not always before) the private interests of Britain.

12. He meant he was determined that when Britain truly believed in a policy it would lead the world in implementing it.

13. They would be expected to trade without taking advantage of the economic weakness of their suppliers and customers. They must not exploit people or the environment.

14. Democracies do not (as a rule) fight each other; and open societies are more likely to be good trade and ideological partners.

15. We cannot hope to change a culture by lecturing it — and anyway, this is an arrogant line to take. Nor do we want the Americans, French and Russians to do the deals that we refuse to do.

Document response

16 Pragmatism is doing what works. It does not neglect principle, but it is more likely to seek compromise than be too high-minded. The pragmatist is inclined to take the line of least resistance.

Essay question

There are obvious A and B positions here:

Position A
GB should not meddle in others' affairs.

Position B
GB has no choice but to be concerned.

These are the points I shall make:

Position A
- Who are we to judge?
- How would we like it if other states meddled in our affairs?
- The 'realists' are right.

Position B
- We value democracy. We cannot, therefore, connive with tyrants at the trampling of democratic rights.
- Open societies are better trading partners.
- National borders are becoming irrelevant.

I take the two positions in this order, because I shall want to agree with the B position.

How far can one culture stand in judgement on another? Was slavery wrong in the newly born United States of America because we say it is wrong now? Were our forebears who believed in the existence of the devil immoral because they believed that those who consorted with the devil should be purged? Were Victorian men unethical because they did not give women the vote? If we wonder whether we should judge other cultures in history, it is much more difficult to answer the question of whether we should judge other cultures in geographical space. The Saudis live by a different law and by different social conventions. Are theirs wrong and ours right? The Chinese say we lay too much emphasis on 'rights' — that this is a western obsession — and that we should stop lecturing them. Could they be right?

Each nation has its own history and its own traditions, and none is in a conspicuously better position to moralise than any other. How would we like it if, for instance, a trading partner lectured us about the British record in Northern Ireland? Or if Arab states broke off trading relations with us because we too readily supported American policy against Saddam Hussein in Iraq and Colonel Gadaffi in Libya? Are we sure that our hands are clean? Perhaps we can really only hope for gradual change — after all, our attitudes in Britain to what is morally acceptable and what is unacceptable undergo constant change. We can expect that standards will evolve elsewhere, too. Meanwhile, there is business to be done; and if we in Britain are so certain — or so priggish — as to climb to the 'moral high ground', we shall find that our competitors in the 'real world' have done business with our customers down on the plain, and had more moral influence into the bargain.

Section 1

> The above arguments might have been telling in the past; but they ought not to convince us now. If we really believe — as we surely do — that factory owners ought not to have forced young children to work at unprotected machines from dawn till dusk, how can we allow British companies to treat the children of other nations in the same way? If we really believe that it was wrong of our forebears to rob the Maoris and Native Americans of their inheritance, how can we sign deals with foreign governments to build dams that will displace minorities against their will? Human rights are the same everywhere.
>
> Besides, doing business with undemocratic regimes is fraught with risk. A tyrant can as well renege on an agreement as sign his name to it. How far can one trust a business partner who does not have the trust of the people? Open societies are progressive societies, permitting free trade, entrepreneurialism and individual initiative. They are societies with effective banking systems and a respect for international norms, for example in the matter of copyright law.
>
> What is more, globalisation is making national borders irrelevant. Companies, currencies, communications are all being internationalised. Acid rain, nuclear radiation, global warming: these do not recognise frontiers; and environmental policies and behaviour are of a piece with policies and behaviour in other fields. A government that lets logging companies ravage its forests is a government that will oppress its people. We have come to understand that we are one world from the natural resources point of view; we have come to recognise the need to bring war criminals to justice in The Hague, and to prevent countries like Serbia bullying its neighbours. It is time to carry concerns in the political and economic spheres into the broader moral sphere, and to accept that we are our brother's keeper. *(619 words)*

AO4 The whole issue is an AO4 issue in that it is about *certainty*, or the lack of it. Ultimately, though, the answer rejects the view that human rights are just a matter of *opinion* or cultural *bias*: 'human rights are the same everywhere'. This is a *fact* of sorts.

Section 1 Social Sciences

Social class

Passage 1: The middle classes in modern Britain

It comes as something of a shock to realise that there are now more university lecturers than coal miners! In 1991, 29.4% of those in the workforce worked in professions and management, a figure only marginally smaller than the 32.7% who worked as manual workers. If one were to include the self-employed (10.7%) and the routine white-collar workers (27.2%) as part of the middle class, we would have to conclude that the middle classes now comprise a substantial majority of the employed population.

Studies of the middle classes have always been bedevilled by the 'boundary problem', the problem of deciding which types of people can helpfully be seen as part of the middle class. In recent years a considerable amount of agreement has been reached on this tricky issue, however. Traditionally, the most common way of differentiating the working classes from the middle classes was to claim that the working class were manual workers, whilst the middle classes were non-manual workers. This difference is occasionally referred to as the 'collar line', the distinction between blue-collar (manual) and white-collar (non-manual) workers. Today, this stress on the collar line has largely been discredited. It is generally agreed that many routine white-collar workers (especially women) now have rather similar conditions of work and remuneration to blue-collar workers, and cannot helpfully be seen as being in a higher class.

The rise in employment in the service sector confuses the division between manual and non-manual workers anyway, and it is possible to argue that many of the most extreme forms of 'proletarianisation' — in the sense of poor wages, irregular employment, and bad working conditions — are found amongst service workers. By the 1980s only 8% of British unskilled workers were employed in industry!

The self-employed also pose interesting puzzles for thinking about the middle classes. Between 1971 and 1981 the numbers of self-employed bottomed out, at around 6.7% of those in the labour market; whilst in the years between 1981 and 1991 the numbers rose by a staggering 45%, to comprise over 10% of the workforce. The difficulty resides, however, in knowing what to make of this rise in numbers. Does it indicate a flourishing petty economy, and the expansion of opportunities for entrepreneurs? Or is there a bleaker portrait to be painted?

In the past self-employment tended not to carry high status, and (with the exception of 'independent' professionals in legal or architectural practice and so on) most professional and managerial employees preferred to achieve rewards and standing by working for a large organisation. This seems to have changed, however. Considerable numbers of managers now seem to prefer to work for small firms or for themselves; and the proportion of managers moving into self-employment rose considerably in the 1980s. Many areas of expanding self-employment were in 'glamorous' areas, such as consultancy work in financial services, or in 'hi-tech' industry.

It seems sensible to see manual workers, the unemployed, and most routine white-collar workers as occupying largely working-class positions, which means that the majority of the population can still usefully be seen as working class (which comprises around 60% of the workforce).

Research on political alignments suggests that the political alignments of the 'salariat' have actually changed little, despite the major political upheavals of recent years. Around 50–55% appear to identify with the Conservative party and around 22% with the Labour party. There are also significant differences within the 'service class'. Public-sector workers tend to be more left-wing than private-sector workers. Welfare and creative workers, such as journalists, teachers, artists and so on are distinctive in being relatively left-wing. The highly educated appear to be more left-wing than the less highly educated, a fact with appears to endorse the 'new class' idea, at least for some fractions of the middle classes.

Source: 'The middle classes in modern Britain', by Mike Savage, SOCIOLOGY REVIEW, Vol.5, No.2, November 1995.

Passage 2: Proletarianisation revisited

The concept of proletarianisation has been defined in several ways. In objective terms it was first used to refer to the likelihood of those from middle-class backgrounds joining the working class through downward social mobility during the course of their working lives. Here the focus is on people, rather than positions. Secondly others have argued that service-sector jobs, especially those occupied by routine white-collar workers, have been de-skilled in terms of job content and routinisation of tasks, so that the jobs are indistinguishable from those of manual workers. Finally, there is the subjective dimension — the extent to which certain middle-class groups within the labour force identify themselves as working class.

Since the post-war expansion of white-collar work, much attention has focused on the precise class position of these employees. David Lockwood analysed the work, market and status situation of clerical workers in Britain. With regard to the work situation, he argued that mechanisation and large modern offices made identification with 'the boss' more difficult. The bureaucratisation of large organisations tended to produce a common identity among clerks.

Document response

Lockwood argued that although the status situation of clerical workers had reduced, it was still higher than that of manual workers; also most clerks did not regard themselves as proletarian. Overall, Lockwood concluded that important differences remained between the two groups and therefore the proletarianisation thesis should be rejected.

This view of clerical work was challenged by Braverman in 1974. The expansion of the clerical sector has been accompanied by increased managerial control over the conception and planning of office work (scientific management) and the extensive use of mechanisation and computerisation. The resultant de-skilling is a process which Braverman believes has created 'an immense mass of wage workers'. He also envisaged the proletarianisation of some professions and semi-professions such as teachers and nurses.

Gallie argues that rather than de-skilling, a process of skill polarisation appears to be taking place within the labour force. Those that already had relatively high levels of skill witnessed an increase in their skill levels, whilst those with low skill levels saw their skills stagnate. This is closely associated with technological change, as the former group of employees are more likely to use advanced technology than the latter. Added to this is the increasing use made by organisations of flexible work practices to enable employers to adjust labour to meet fluctuations in demand. Part-time work, temporary contracts, consultancies and subcontracting are making the practice of a 'job for life' less likely for both blue- and white-collar workers. Such changes mean that employment becomes less secure for these employees compared to those with full-time, permanent contracts, who frequently form a core workforce of well-paid and highly trained employees.

Routine clerical employees, men and women, tend to describe themselves as 'middle class' rather than 'working class'. They are also less likely to belong to a trade union than members of the manual working class and to be more likely to vote Conservative than Labour. However, if we look at public-sector professions and semi-professions such as nurses, social workers and teachers, we can see increasing electoral support for the Labour party. In recent years they have experienced a lowering of their rewards and an increase in managerial control, which has reduced their professional autonomy. Pressure towards the routinisation of work is evident. The nursing profession has faced an increased through-put of patients, a growing demand for routine recording of data and the growth of contracts which specify precise tasks and duties.

As we have seen, public-sector professional and clerical positions are showing some signs of proletarianisation, but there are still huge differences between these positions and those in the manual sector. The former still enjoy better life-chances, promotion prospects, fringe benefits and higher status. Subjectively, there seems to be little evidence that non-manual workers see themselves as working class.

Source: 'Proletarianisation revisited', by Jane Clarke, SOCIOLOGY REVIEW, Vol.5, No.2, November 1995.

Section 1

Multiple-choice questions

Passage 1: The middle classes in modern Britain

1 The fact that there are more lecturers than miners comes as a 'shock' because:
   A   The economy needs coal miners more than university lecturers.
   B   It had been thought that manual workers outnumber élite professionals.
   C   It emphasises what an explosion there has been in the university sector.
   D   We do not think of university lecturers as belonging to the working class.

2 Until recently the working class was defined so as to include:
   A   Only blue-collar, manual workers.
   B   All blue-collar and female white-collar workers.
   C   White-collar workers doing routine jobs.
   D   Manual workers, blue-collar and white-collar.

3 'Proletarianisation' refers to:
   (i)   The growing number of workers in the service sectors of the economy.
   (ii) Working-class pay and conditions spreading to 'middle-class' jobs.
   (iii) The growth of political consciousness among the working classes.
   (iv) Increasing trade-union militancy among non-manual workers.

   Answer:
   A   if (i) only is correct.
   B   if (ii) and (iii) are correct.
   C   if (ii) only is correct.
   D   if all are correct.

4 The problem posed for sociologists by the rise of self-employment is:
   A   Knowing whether people choose to be self-employed or not.
   B   Knowing whether or not this means the end of the large organisation.
   C   Understanding how far this affects only management personnel.
   D   Deciding whether this represents a worsening of conditions for this group.

5 The author, in this article, places routine white-collar workers:
   A   In the middle class along with a substantial majority of the population.
   B   In the working class along with manual workers and the unemployed.
   C   Tentatively in the middle class, then subsequently in the working class.
   D   In a class of their own, since they wear neither blue nor white collars.

Passage 2: Proletarianisation revisited

6 That certain service-sector jobs have been 'de-skilled' means that:
   A   They have become manual jobs as in the manufacturing sector.
   B   It is no longer necessary to be a member of the middle class to do such work.
   C   The work is routine and rather menial.
   D   They are occupied by people who had considered themselves middle-class.

Document response

7 'Bureaucratisation' (l. 14) means:
  A The growth of departmentalism, hierarchies and routine paperwork.
  B The unionisation and politicisation of employees.
  C The growing numbers of female white-collar employees in companies.
  D The extent to which clerical workers are suffering downward mobility.

8 'Skill polarisation' (l. 28) is taking place as a result of:
  (i)   The increasing use of advanced technology.
  (ii) The growth of casual and part-time work.
  (iii) The adoption by employers of flexible work practices.
  (iv) The general upward mobility of manual workers.

  Answer:
  A if (i) only is correct.   C if (i), (ii) and (iii) are correct.
  B if (i) and (ii) only are correct. D if all are correct.

9 In recent years teachers have:
  A Taken on more managerial, and fewer professional, tasks.
  B Begun to think of themselves as members of the working class.
  C Enjoyed higher pay levels since they joined unions.
  D Suffered a certain loss of professional status.

10 NHS nurses:
  A Still enjoy more benefits than working-class manual workers.
  B Now regard themselves as occupying routine, working-class jobs.
  C Have resisted attempts to challenge their professional autonomy.
  D Suffered a serious reduction in income during the recession.

Short-answer questions (Passages 1 and 2)

11 Both passages are about social class — rather, both are about a particular problem in the study of social class. What is that problem?

12 What do both passages appear to acknowledge has happened to much white-collar, 'middle-class' work in recent years?

13 What does the writer of Passage 1 have to say about the 'collar line' that the writer of Passage 2 makes no reference to?

14 On which definition of 'proletarianisation' do both writers appear to agree?

15 What other definitions of 'proletarianisation' does Passage 2 supply that are absent from Passage 1?

16 Both passages refer to the changing nature of much white-collar work. What is one of the causes of the change, referred to in Passage 2, and what effect is it said to have had?

Section 1

17 In what respect(s) do the two passages agree about middle-class voting patterns?

18 In what respect(s) is the writer of Passage 1 more optimistic about the self-employed than the writer of Passage 2?

Essay question

Comment on the view that Britain is no longer a country divided on social-class lines.

Answers

1 (b) The common perception is that university lecturers are an élite group ('dons'), few in number in comparison with 'humble' miners. Of course, universities have grown in number as the number of mines has dramatically shrunk.

2 (a) Routine white-collar work has generally been thought of as middle-class.

3 (c) (ii) is correct. Proletarianisation refers to working-class pay and conditions — unionisation, lower status, more routine, less autonomy, stagnant rates of pay — spreading to 'middle-class' jobs such as clerical, teaching, nursing.

4 (d) The problem is deciding whether self-employment is beneficial overall, or whether it represents a worsening of conditions (the loss of the 'job for life', in the words of Passage 2).

5 (c) Tentatively in the middle class (paragraph 1), then subsequently in the working class (paragraph 6).

6 (c) The jobs have not, of course, become manual in any literal sense — answer (a).

7 (a) *Bureau* is the French for 'office'; bureaucracy is form-filling, filing, paper-shuffling and playing by office rules.

8 (c) Computerisation divides the workforce into 'cans' and 'cannots' (i); casualisation distinguishes between the non-voluntarily part-time and the voluntarily freelance (ii); and employers exploit this distinction (iii).

9 (d) '…they have experienced a lowering of their rewards and an increase in managerial control' over their work. Hence, a loss of the autonomy that is the hallmark of the professional.

10 (a) '…better life-chances, promotion prospects, fringe benefits and higher status'.

11 The problem is how to distinguish between the middle and working classes, given the continual background of social change.

12 They agree that much white-collar work has become routinised; there is less skill involved, there is lower status and less job security.

Document response

13 The writer of Passage 1 refers to the 'collar line' as a 'discredited' index of difference, i.e. it is no longer considered valid. The writer of Passage 2 uses the terms without making this comment.

14 They agree that there has been a proletarianisation of much 'middle-class' work in its routinisation, its de-skilling and its downgrading of status.

15 The writer of Passage 2 refers to individual downward mobility of members of the middle class; and to the extent to which such members come to perceive themselves, subjectively, to be of the working class.

16 One of the causes of the change is advanced technology: it has divided employees into those who can use it to the full and those for whom it is only a small or routine part of their work.

17 They agree that public-sector workers, and in particular the educated professionals and semi-professionals, tend to vote Labour.

18 The writer of Passage 1 recognises that many employees choose to deny themselves a 'job for life'; that self-employment is their preferred option because it gives them professional autonomy — and many enjoy high status.

Essay question

There are obvious A and B positions here:

Position A
Britain is divided on social-class lines.

Position B
Britain is not divided on social-class lines.

In the A position, one would have to show that social class is still a factor. Class still has a bearing on the types of school that children attend, for example. But 'class' is too blunt a scalpel nowadays. There are many other factors that play a part in the roles we occupy. We are not only defined by our jobs. Besides, we have much more choice of (a) how to live ('lifestyle'), (b) where to live and (c) what to do for a living, than used to be the case.

I shall conclude that a straightforward division of Britons into two or three classes is facile and inadequate.

Time was when we could talk significantly of three classes in Britain: of a small upper class who owned a disproportionate amount of national wealth; a larger middle class (or classes) of professionals, businessmen and skilled craftsmen; and a large working class (or classes). The division was quite static before the First World War. There was some mobility between the wars and after the Second World War — but even in the mid- to late-1950s, young men could be 'angry' because their (provincial) university education did not give them access to 'establishment' jobs.

There is still a distinctly 'upper-class' flavour about many British institutions: Henley Royal Regatta, Ascot Races, Cowes, the Badminton Horse Trials, polo, fox-hunting, the Lords Members' Room, shopping at Harrods, dining at the Ritz, and first nights at Covent Garden. There are still upper-class places to live (Virginia Water, Eaton Square, Alderley Edge, Edgbaston) and upper-class places to spend your holidays (almost anywhere inaccessible to package holidays) and send your children to school.

Middle-class institutions are rather harder to define. Are you middle-class if you read a broadsheet newspaper, drive the children to school in a Range Rover, holiday on 'unspoilt' Mediterranean beaches, work in a rather smart office, live in a 'nice' neighbourhood, and drink Beaujolais from Oddbins rather than Carling Black Label in four-packs from Tesco's? The indicators of class have been rather muddled in recent years. It is still probably true, though, that one's education indicates one's parents' class aspirations, reinforces one's own class identity and powerfully influences one's class affiliation in adulthood. If one goes to Industrial Terrace Secondary Modern School it is likely that one's parents went there, that they know no better, that one's chances of going to Balliol College are limited, and that one's career opportunities will be stunted. Children who go to such a school will not mind, because their friends are there and they feel culturally at home.

This, however, is perhaps a caricature from the 1950s. There are mercifully few secondary modern schools left. The 'comprehensive' reorganisation of the 1960s largely put an end to the institutional perpetuation of class divisions at the age of 11. It may still be much more difficult for an 8-year-old from Barnsley to enter Balliol than his or her counterpart from semi-rural Bucks. — but no comprehensive-school student need be a Jude the Obscure. Besides, such a student may be quite undazzled by life in a college quad: not only may one aspire to the City, or the Bench, or the boardroom, or High Table with a degree from any one of a number of excellent universities untouched by social snobbery, but one may hope to occupy No. 10 Downing Street or the chief executive's office of a Footsie-quoted company without having been to university at all.

It is not just that one can be a premier-league footballer, a tone-deaf musician or an 'Internet nerd' to take home a 6-figure salary; it is that we are no longer defined socially by the jobs that we do. How we live, where we live and what we do for a living have simply ceased to be indicators of anything very much beyond personal preference. To be sure, there are still housing estates and family estates — but in between, the variety of 'lifestyles' is such as (almost) to defy categorisation. The National Lottery creates a millionaire every week — and the keenest punters are skilled manual workers.

(569 words)

AO4 Again, this is an essentially AO4 topic because it is less about *facts* than about perception and *beliefs*. The *evidence* base is mostly *soft*. Nevertheless, all the 'indicators' referred to are factual evidence of a sort.

That I used a word like 'mercifully' demonstrates that I am not altogether *impartial*.

Section 1 Sciences

Air pollution and asthma

Air pollution and asthma

Asthma is now one of the commonest diseases in industrialised countries. It affects over 10% of children and 5–10% of adults, and accumulating evidence from around the world points to a steady increase in the number of cases. Many articles have been written in the mass media on the possible contribution of air pollution to the increased prevalence of asthma. While there is no convincing support for the idea that the worldwide increase in asthma is caused by air pollution, there is increasing evidence that air pollution may contribute to an increase in asthma symptoms.

Discussions about air pollution tend to focus on events outdoors but several potentially dangerous pollutants can be found indoors — including environmental tobacco smoke, allergens derived from house dust mites and pet fur, and nitrogen dioxide (NO_2) generated by gas appliances. For example, there is some evidence that gas cookers are associated with increased symptoms in asthmatic patients. However, most concern has focused on whether *outdoor* air pollution, particularly that generated by road traffic, is increasing asthma symptoms.

Several pollutants are present in outdoor air. Vehicle exhaust fumes contain oxides of nitrogen (mainly NO_2), of sulphur (mainly SO_2), minute particles which can be inhaled (referred to as particulate matter — PM_{10}). Diesel particulates are of particular concern as the small particles may reach the gas exchanging surface of the lung and cause inflammation of the lung and the airways. Ozone (O_3) is a secondary pollutant, which is formed by the action of sunlight on oxides of nitrogen in the presence of hydrocarbons. The formation of ozone is favoured by warm temperatures, sunlight and low winds. Once formed, ozone may be carried long distances by prevailing winds. Ozone is broken down in the presence of NO, so that its concentration in cities may be *less* than in rural areas.

There have been recent changes in the nature of air pollution in industrialised countries, with a decline in the levels of SO_2 and smoke created by the burning of fossil fuels, but there has been an increase in the levels of NO_2, O_3 and diesel particulates, resulting from increases in the density of road traffic.

It has proved difficult to establish a firm link between traffic pollution and asthma. It is possible that air pollution may *cause* asthma by increasing the risk of developing asthma in someone with an allergic disposition, thus leading to an increase in the number of patients with asthma in the community. However, it is more likely that air pollution increases symptoms in individuals who are already asthmatic. Although there has been a lot of research into this, the evidence is conflicting. This is partly because of the difficulty in establishing a clear association between air pollution and asthma symptoms, as there are several confounding factors.

It is possible that pollutants and allergens may have a greater effect in combination but there is no convincing evidence that air pollution is related to the prevalence of asthma. Asthma is no more common in urban populations (where levels of air pollution would be expected to be higher) than in rural communities in industrialised countries.

The reunification of Germany has provided data on two populations exposed to very different types of air pollution. East German industrialised towns, such as Leipzig and Erfurt, have high levels of SO_2 and particulates in the air, whereas West German cities, such as Munich and Hamburg, have low levels of SO_2 and particulates, but higher levels of NO_2. The prevalence of asthma and allergic diseases is higher in Munich than in Leipzig, but the prevalence of bronchitis is higher in Leipzig. Similarly, there is a much higher frequency of reported asthma attacks in Hamburg than in Erfurt. There is also a higher prevalence of sensitisation to indoor allergens in schoolchildren from former East Germany, although there is no difference in sensitivity to outdoor allergens. All of this suggests that indoor exposure to allergens is a more important determinant of asthma than exposure to outdoor air pollutants, such as SO_2 and particulates.

Source: 'Air pollution and asthma', by Peter Barnes, BIOLOGICAL SCIENCES REVIEW, Vol.9, No.4, March 1997.

Multiple-choice questions

1 Articles in the mass media have:
  A Demonstrated a clear link between asthma and air pollution.
  B Expressed doubt as to whether there is any connection between air pollution and asthma.
  C Hypothesised a correlation between levels of air pollution and asthma.
  D Exploited public concern about rising levels of air pollution.

2 Pollution in the domestic environment:
  A Has been discounted as an aggravating factor in the incidence of asthma.
  B May well have a part to play in the increase of asthma symptoms.
  C Is principally the result of defective domestic gas appliances.
  D Is of rather less importance than pollution from vehicle exhausts.

3 Diesel particulates give cause for concern because:
  A They may be implicated in the more serious respiratory problems.
  B The number of diesel vehicles on the road is growing all the time.
  C They are so minute that asthma sufferers are not aware of them.
  D They have been shown to cause a particularly acute form of asthma.

Document response

4 The problem of determining the correlation between air pollution and asthma is that:
  A Many patients undergoing treatment had asthma already.
  B External pollution may compound asthma contracted indoors.
  C The results of one research study contradict those of another.
  D It is difficult to disentangle and control all the variables.

5 Comparison between East and West Germany offers us:
  A Two populations having different histories of air pollution.
  B Neighbours exposed by their governments to different pathogens.
  C Two societies subject to the same sorts of industrial pollution.
  D Peoples exposed to the same external, but different internal environments.

Short-answer questions

6 Why should there be so much 'public concern' about an increase in asthma symptoms?

7 Why do you think most of this concern has focused on pollution in the outdoor environment?

8 Why may one not be protected from ozone by living in the countryside?

9 What has brought about a decline in the incidence of sulphur dioxide in the atmosphere in western Europe?

10 What seems to be meant by someone's having an 'allergic disposition'?

11 How might we account for the fact that, in industrialised countries, asthma is no more prevalent in urban than in rural areas?

12 Why might children in eastern Germany suffer from greater sensitisation to indoor allergens than children from western Germany?

Short-essay question

Identify and comment upon policies that might be pursued to reduce levels of pollution in the external environment.

Answers

1 (c) The media may have exploited public concern — (d) — but there is no warrant for this in the text.

2 (b) The final sentence of the text makes it clear that domestic pollution may play the major part.

3 (a) They may be to blame for lung and windpipe damage, giving rise to breathing problems. Answer (d) is too strong. Hard evidence is not yet available (or wasn't at the time of writing).

4 **(d)** There evidently is no one-to-one relationship between air pollution and asthma. Factors may work in complex combination.

5 **(a)** There have been different policies on the burning of fossil fuels by industry, and different levels and sources of traffic pollution.

6 The rise in asthma suffering has been rather sudden and evident — particularly among children — at a time when we are all more conscious of the multiple effects of traffic density.

7 Individuals can do rather little to influence the outdoor environment, whereas — in theory, at least — they can control the indoor environment by not smoking, not keeping pets and so on.

8 Once the ozone has formed in city areas it is taken elsewhere by the wind, where it is less likely to be broken down by nitrogen oxides.

9 There has been less burning of the fossil fuels that produce sulphur dioxide — particularly coal — in the west. Much low-grade brown coal is still burnt in eastern Europe.

10 Someone who has an 'allergic disposition' has a natural sensitivity to allergy-causing factors (allergens) in the environment. They are particularly susceptible to allergies.

11 We might account for this by the action of the wind in taking pollution a long way from its source, or by the fact that indoor pollution is the real culprit.

12 Children in eastern Germany may be sensitised to indoor pollutants by the higher incidence of SO_2 and particulates in the external environment; or gas appliances in eastern Germany may be to blame.

Short-essay question

> There is really no pair of positions here — conflicting or complementary. This is the sort of essay title that calls for a list of (in this case) policies. It scarcely matters about their order.
>
> I shall refer separately to measures to tackle vehicle pollution and industrial pollution.

There can be little doubt that vehicle pollution is an irritant to those who are prone to asthma, and we are all more or less susceptible to the effects of breathing polluted air. It must, therefore, be any government's objective to reduce unnecessary vehicle use; to insist that vehicles be as pollution-free as may be; and to encourage transport systems that carry the maximum number of passengers per unit of fuel consumed. Motorists and companies using lorries and vans must be provided with realistic, efficient alternatives if they are to be persuaded to use public transport. In urban areas, light rapid-transit systems are relatively energy-efficient.

Document response

Lean-burn engines and catalytic converters should be adopted as standard. Diesel fuel was thought to be 'greener' than unleaded petrol — but there is now doubt about this. Particulates are not easily captured by filters that are currently available and in use. Electric cars are an attractive idea: but the electricity still has to be generated somewhere. Vegetable alcohol-fuelled cars are another possibility; but perhaps solar-powered vehicles are least likely of all to compromise the quality of the air we breathe. A solar-powered car has been tested in Australia, and solar-powered buses are in prospect.

The atmosphere above our industrial cities has certainly improved since the end of the days of intensive coal-burning. Gone are the 'pea-soup' fogs of old. Natural gas is a non-renewable fossil fuel, but the 'dash for gas' has undoubtedly contributed to less discharge of greenhouse gas into the atmosphere. It would be good to be able to give nuclear energy a clean bill of health, since it is non-polluting — other than in terms (very significantly) of the waste for which we really have no answer. Perhaps we shall have to live with this problem until viable renewable sources of energy are fully harnessed. Wind energy, in particular, is deserving of much higher levels of investment in Britain, particularly in offshore stations.

All factory flues should be fitted with sulphur filters to combat acid rain; and all other forms of atmospheric pollution should be discouraged, according to the 'polluter pays' principle, in such a way as to make it more costly to discharge pollutants than to invest in technology that is (at least relatively) clean. *(373 words)*

AO4 There would not seem to be much room for AO4 debate here — yet it is about *evidence* (of the cleanness or otherwise of diesel fuel, for example); and it is certainly about *values*. It is about whether we value health above mobility, or vice versa.

Section 1 Sciences

Transgenic pigs

Transgenic pigs — human organ factories?

The success of organ transplant operations is attributed to the development of drugs that suppress the immune system to prevent or control rejection of the organ. So successful are these procedures, and so great is the demand for transplantation to improve the life expectancy of patients with kidney, heart or liver failure, that there is now a worldwide organ shortage.

Various strategies have been developed in an effort to meet the increasing demand for organs for transplantation. These include the development of artificial organs and attempts to increase the supply of human organs by educating people about the value and success of donor transplants. In spite of the networks and mechanisms set in place in Europe and the USA to maximise the availability of organs for transplantation, the demand far outstrips the supply of donor organs.

This shortage has led scientists to conclude that only a new source of organs can overcome this problem. Research programmes specifically focused on the construction of artificial organs have started in several countries. Although this approach could represent a solution for organs whose primary role is essentially mechanical (e.g. the heart, the function of which is to pump blood around the body), it does not seem to be applicable for organs, such as the liver and kidney, that depend on the more complex biological activities of their cells to fulfil their functions. Researchers have therefore started to concentrate on trying to transplant organs from other species (*xenotransplantation*).

If xenotransplantation were to become a reality, it would be possible to solve the organ shortage problem by breeding animals to provide an unlimited supply of organs of any size for human transplantation. Also, it would allow transplantation to become a reality for the large number of high-risk patients for whom, presently, organs are not made available. The current high costs of transplantation associated with operations on donors and recipients at different locations could also be dramatically reduced.

The pig is regarded as the most suitable donor for xenotransplantation into humans. Pigs are physiologically and anatomically similar to man. They breed easily, have fairly short pregnancies and give birth to large litters of offspring which grow rapidly to a size at which their organs are suitable for human transplantation. A recent working party established by the Nuffield Council on Bioethics to consider xenotransplantation concluded that the use of pigs did not raise the same ethical issues that could arise from the use of organs from non-human primates. The greater intelligence and complexity of social interactions of the higher primates persuaded the working party that it might not be ethically acceptable to use these animals for this purpose. The genetic similarity of humans and non-human primates also suggested to the working party that there might be a greater danger of introducing a new disease by transmission of an infectious organism from primate to human. Moreover, this approach would require a substantial breeding programme to be set up.

Transplantation of organs from standard domestic pigs into humans would rapidly lead to the loss of the graft by an immunological phenomenon called *hyperacute rejection*. This response currently represents the biggest obstacle to xenotransplantations of pig organs into humans. It results from a very aggressive reaction of the recipient's immune system towards the pig tissue, which is recognised as foreign to the body. This immune response involves the production by the recipient of antibodies against antigens on the surface of the foreign tissue.

Modern advances in molecular biology now make it possible to consider ways around this problem.

Source: 'Transgenic pigs — human organ factories?', by Emanuele Cozzi and David White, BIOLOGICAL SCIENCES REVIEW, Vol.9, No.2, November 1996.

Multiple-choice questions

1 Organ transplants have been so successful because:
  A They have been given so much publicity in the newspapers.
  B They have become a matter of simple, surgical routine.
  C There is such a huge demand owing to organ failure.
  D Drugs have been developed that inhibit the normal rejection process.

2 An education programme has attempted to:
  A Persuade recipients that transplant surgery is safe.
  B Raise the awareness of potential organ donors to the need.
  C Give publicity to the successful development of artificial organs.
  D Encourage people to join networks of organ donors.

3 Research into the development of artificial organs is under way to:
  A Overcome the problem of the shortage of donor organs.
  B Focus attention on the success of organ transplant surgery.
  C Perfect the operation of artificial kidneys and livers.
  D Mitigate the effects of rejection of donor tissue.

4 Xenotransplantation is:
  A The transplantation of organs from one human to another.
  B Organ transplantation between non-human animals.

C   The transplanting of organs from non-human animals to humans.
D   The development of artificial organs in non-human animals.

5 Pigs are especially suitable donors inasmuch as:
A   They are prolific and are biologically similar to humans.
B   We have long experience of breeding pigs for their meat.
C   We do not have any moral scruples about killing pigs.
D   Pigs are intelligent and engage in complex social interactions.

6 Primates are thought not to be suitable because:
A   They are not physiologically and anatomically similar to humans.
B   It is ethically unacceptable to exploit highly evolved species.
C   Human societies have greatly reduced the numbers of higher primates.
D   The great apes do not breed easily and have long pregnancies.

7 The big problem where xenotransplantation is concerned is that:
A   The general public rejects the idea of receiving organs from pigs.
B   There is no way to overcome the rejection of foreign tissue.
C   The immune systems of pigs produce powerful antibodies.
D   It is necessary to overcome immunological hyperacute rejection.

Short-answer questions

8 Why do you suppose there is such a demand for replacement organs?

9 What is the purpose of the 'networks and mechanisms' (ll. 9–10) that have been put in place in Europe and the USA?

10 Why is an artificial heart likely to be more effective than an artificial kidney?

11 Who are likely to be the 'high-risk' patients referred to in l. 24?

12 Why might xenotransplantation reduce the current high costs of organ transplantation?

13 What might be meant by the 'complexity of social interactions' (l. 35) among non-human primates?

14 Why would it be more complicated to set up a primate- than a pig-breeding programme?

Essay question

'To breed pigs purely for them to supply us with replacement organs is immoral.' Imagine that you are a doctor who believes in xenotransplantation, and write a reply to this statement.

Document response

Answers

1 **(d)** Answers (a) and (b) are not causes of success — they are effects.

2 **(b)** The programme has raised the awareness of potential donors to the need for them to carry donor cards, and to the need for everyone to be prepared to donate and allow relatives to 'donate' should the latter die unexpectedly.

3 **(a)** But artificial organs are not the ideal solution. We are unlikely to be able to simulate the action of kidneys and livers — answer (c).

4 **(c)** It is transplantation across the species boundary. We are unlikely to want to do it in reverse.

5 **(a)** We presumably have some scruples about killing pigs — (c); and the (d) descriptor refers to higher primates.

6 **(b)** It would be ethically unsuitable to exploit them for this or any other purpose. Answer (a) is the opposite of the case, and, whilst (c) is undoubtedly true, this is not the reason for our scruples.

7 **(d)** Answer (a) may be true, but is not the 'big problem'. As regards (b), it would appear that there is a way of overcoming this problem; and (c) — it is the human recipient who produces the antibodies.

8 The success of the operation has stimulated some of the demand. As people live healthier lives, the failure of one or another organ is more obviously a factor in decline — so the remedy is more obvious, too. Our expectation of long life and successful remediation is also higher.

9 These networks and mechanisms are designed to speed the traffic of organs from donors to recipients over sometimes quite long distances.

10 A heart is simply a blood-pump; it is not a particularly complex organ, so it can be simulated relatively easily. The liver and kidneys are the seat of complicated chemical activity.

11 They are patients whose organ failure is acute, who cannot survive the wait for an appropriate organ, or organs; or those for whom a traumatic operation might only further endanger their lives.

12 These costs are partly the result of the distance in time and space. Pigs' organs could be ready (on the hoof), close to the point of need.

13 The higher primates engage in affective relationships with each other of a more nearly human kind than those (apparently) engaged in by pigs.

14 The higher primates are not native to the European and American locations where it is most likely such operations would be carried out. Furthermore, they are less naturally fertile than pigs.

Section 1

Essay question

Though you favour xenotransplantation (for the purposes of this essay), you will still need to acknowledge the arguments of those who oppose it. This is Position A. Your case for xenotransplantation is Position B:

Position A
Reasons that might be given for saying xenotransplantation is immoral

Position B
Reasons why it may be considered moral

Essentially, the B position is based on a human preference for human over non-human life. A doctor could hardly argue otherwise. S/he might also be expected to argue that — unless we are vegetarians or vegans — we accept animal breeding and slaughter for less vital purposes than xenotransplantation.

It may be thought that xenotransplantation involves cruelty to animals. Were this the case then it would certainly be immoral, even if that cruelty was not wanton and arbitrary, but systematic. It would be the aim of the medical profession to keep pigs in humane conditions, and to terminate their lives only when there was an urgent need for their organs. It may be objected that we ought not to be so callous as to exploit a species in this way — to use it as a means to human ends. This would certainly be the view of the philosopher Peter Singer, who believes that our exploitation of animals for food is on a par with the exploitation of black West Africans by white slavers at the end of the eighteenth century. He refers to this discrimination against animals as 'speciesism'. Only a vegan or vegetarian (like Singer) can argue consistently from this position. If we eat meat — even if we keep cows for their milk (and cheese, and other milk products) — we act as if we believe that human life is of more importance than animal life. To this extent, xenotransplantation is no more immoral than meat-eating. Most people do not think meat-eating is immoral; therefore — it may be assumed — the breeding of pigs for selective killing, as and when a human life is endangered, can only consistently be considered immoral by a minority of principled vegans.

Breeding pigs genetically engineered is really no more morally challenging than breeding them so as to maximise their lean meat, body weight or fertility for the ultimate purpose of slaughtering them and eating them. How many of us would say that when a relative of ours is dying for want of a kidney, and no human kidney donor is found, the relative's life is not worth more than that of a single pig? To be sure, we find it easier to contemplate the killing of a 'dirty' and not very physically prepossessing animal than we would of a domestic pet, or furry and 'charming' animal. No respecter of animals would want to underestimate the value of a pig's life to a pig (and certainly not merely because it is a 'pig', and not a penguin); but no doctor, committed to the health of human patients, could not set the life of one such patient above the life of a pig.

Document response

Once we have established that we have the means to hand to reduce the risk of tissue rejection — and it appears that we have — and once we have bred pigs from which suitable organs could be xenotransplanted, the actual breeding programme should not present difficulties. Pigs are the ideal species for all the reasons advanced by Cozzi and White: they are fertile, and grow to such a size as to offer organs of appropriate dimensions for human use. Non-human primates would have to be of a similar size to be suitable — but these would have to be fully grown apes, much higher on the ladder of evolution than pigs. That is to say they share some of the characteristics of a person in that they have a consciousness of their own past and future, and are capable of taking the interests of others into account. To this extent, the higher apes have a higher claim to 'personhood' than human infants and the mentally incapacitated. Pigs, for all their qualities, do not have such a claim.

Pigs not bred for the purpose of xenotransplantation (or the bacon factory) would not be bred at all. It is a matter that goes far beyond the competence of doctors to judge whether it would be better not to live at all than to live well for a while — perhaps a long while — and to die humanely to save a human life. Many a human might wish for as much. *(642 words)*

A04 This is an ethical-philosophical matter quite as much as it is a scientific one. Account is taken, for example, of the *values* of vegetarians and vegans, and of the less-principled (*biased*) value that we may place on the life of a penguin that we would not place on the life of a pig. Science is not all *facts*; there is plenty of room for judgement, too.

Section 1 Sciences

Obesity

Passage 1: Don't blame the metabolism

In 1995 newspapers in America reported that the fattest man in the world had died weighing 465 kilograms — 73 stone. On visits to hospital he had to be transported on a fork-lift truck, and after his death they had to demolish the bedroom wall to remove his body. To some it is perhaps not surprising that this happened in the US, a country with a reputation for excess. But in terms of our metabolism — the rate at which our bodies use energy from food — the excess was not very great. If he started out as a 70 kilogram man aged 16, he would only have needed to gain 37 grams per day to reach his final weight by the time he was 45. This is the equivalent to eating 1.4 megajoules (335 kcal) too much — less than a bar of chocolate, every day. This is an extreme case. Most of us regulate our body weight much more tightly.

The growing number of people becoming obese shows that, despite an aggressive slimming industry, our sedentary lifestyle and high-fat diet are taking their toll.

So what causes obesity? The simple, but facile, answer is 'eating too much'. But if this is the case, why do many people possess inherent control systems which regulate their body weight with such remarkable precision? What is it that has broken down in seriously obese people and makes them keep eating more than they need? We still seem to be some way off answering all these questions, but progress is being made.

One of the biggest difficulties is that obesity has many different causes. There are some well-defined metabolic causes of obesity, though they are extremely rare. One example is Prader Willi syndrome, in which children have insatiable appetites. We are also learning to distinguish psychological causes of obesity, such as the newly classified 'binge eating disorder'.

We also know that there are genetic factors involved. Research shows that, in about a quarter of cases, obesity can be attributed to a person's genetic make-up. The genetics are not simple and probably result from a variety of minor gene effects which occur in a variety of combinations in different individuals. Obesity in Britain is increasing so fast that it cannot possibly be explained by major changes in the gene pool; this shows that most of the obesity has to be non-genetic in origin. The critical external influences include a high-fat diet and our modern sedentary lifestyle.

It is incredibly difficult to measure a person's true food intake. The double-labelled water technique made it possible to cross-check measures of food intake by comparing the results with people's normal levels of energy usage. In people who stay the same weight, for example, energy intake and expenditure should agree. They frequently do not match up, particularly in many obese people who under-record their food intake by quite astonishing amounts. We know this by comparing their food intake records with the double-labelled water measures of energy expenditure. In lean people the values agree very well, but in the obese the apparent food intakes come out much lower than their objective measures of energy expenditure.

Other experiments involve feeding people the same amount of energy that they claim to be eating in normal life. When we do this with obese people they rapidly lose weight because their initial records of food intake were too low. Whether this is a genuine mistake, or deliberate attempt to avoid embarrassment, we do not know. What we have found is that the seemingly trivial act of measuring food intake is one of the most challenging faced by researchers and is a major barrier to progress in many areas of nutrition.

People with AIDS can suffer quite the opposite problem — they apparently eat adequately and yet still lose weight. The theory had been the exact reverse of that in obesity — that the cause was an overactive (i.e. inefficient) metabolism, induced by the disease.

Our double-labelled water technique firmly refuted the faulty metabolism hypothesis. The weight loss was caused by not eating enough of the right foods and not, as had been suspected, by an overactive metabolism. By removing the 'blame it on the metabolism' excuse, we have been able to refocus attention on the importance of diet and nutritional support, and on the psychology of eating — when and why.

Source: 'Don't blame the metabolism', by Andrew Prentice, BIOLOGICAL SCIENCES REVIEW, Vol.9, No.2, November 1996.

Passage 2: Obesity: a weighty problem

Obese people were once regarded as jolly, healthy people, and in some cultures even regarded as beautiful. Identification of health risks associated with obesity has changed our perception. Now the obese person also has the psychological problems of dealing with the social stigma of an unacceptable body image.

Obesity is defined by means of the *body mass index* (*BMI*) — the body mass (kg) divided by the square of the height (m^2). For a typical person of body mass 70 kg and height 1.7 m the BMI is 24.2 kg m^{-2}. An obese person would have a BMI ranging from 30 upwards.

The proportion of adults who are overweight or obese is rising sharply in most developed countries. Currently, about 30% of adults in Britain are overweight while one in six is obese. Predictions suggest that by 2005 about 20% of men and

23% of women in the UK will be obese. In the USA it has been predicted that, if current trends continue, 100% of the population will be obese by the year 2230!

Humans obtain energy from food and use it to carry out the processes essential for life, and also to do other useful work. Energy intake and output are related by the *energy balance equation*:

energy intake = energy expenditure + energy stored

If the energy taken in is greater than the energy expended, there will be an increase in the body's energy stores. Conversely, if energy expenditure exceeds intake then there will be a loss of energy stores.

There are a number of ways in which the body stores energy. These include heat energy (reflected in body temperature — we are warm-blooded) and chemical energy in the form of carbohydrate (glycogen) and fat (triacylglycerol in adipose tissue). The glycogen stores are relatively small and limited, and body temperature remains within narrow limits. Therefore, long-term changes in the body's energy stores reflect changes in the amount of triacylglycerol stored in adipose tissue. This is why we refer to someone who is obese as 'fat'.

Obesity results when energy intake has been consistently greater than energy expenditure. The energy expenditure of obese people is greater than that of lean people. Therefore it is clear that (on average) obese people remain obese because they eat more than lean people.

This statement needs careful interpretation. We do not know what the first trigger is for obesity to develop. It could be that a true metabolic defect in energy expenditure is the first step in becoming obese. There is some evidence from obese animals that appetite and food intake increase simply *as a result of* increased body fat.

People who have a problem controlling their weight would love to believe that it is all fixed by their genes and that there is nothing they can do about it. However, obesity has increased so rapidly that it cannot be explained by genes alone — there must be some interaction between the genetic background of the individual and the environment. The evidence from several studies of identical and non-identical twins (who share 100% and 50% of the same genes respectively) suggests that about 30–40% of the variability in BMI is inherited, the remainder being due to environmental influences.

Environmental influences will include social pressures to eat or not to eat, and to exercise or not exercise. However predisposed to obesity someone might be by their genes, they can only become obese by eating too much in relation to their energy expenditure.

If the environment is responsible for the present increase in obesity, what aspect of the environment is involved? There are probably two factors. One is the present ready availability of food, and particularly food rich in fat. Fat-rich foods are very *energy-dense* — a small amount provides a lot of energy. Unfortunately, they also taste nice! (Would you rather eat 'low-fat' ice cream or rich dairy ice cream?) The other factor is a general decrease in physical activity. Nowadays many journeys are made by car which, earlier this century, would have been walked or bicycled. Children spend long hours in front of a television or computer when previously they might have been out playing football.

The treatment of obesity is simple in principle but incredibly difficult in practice. In principle all that is needed is for the affected person to reduce energy intake, or increase energy expenditure (or both) so that the *energy stored* part of the energy balance equation becomes consistently negative. However, as almost everyone who has tried to lose weight knows, this is easier said than done.

Source: 'Obesity: a weighty problem', by Keith Frayn, BIOLOGICAL SCIENCES REVIEW, Vol.10 No.1, September 1997.

Multiple-choice questions

Passage 1: Don't blame the metabolism

1 The key point being made in paragraph 1 is that:
  A Americans daily take in much more energy than they expend.
  B To cause obesity, the daily excess of energy does not have to be great.
  C Americans have a daily excess of energy equivalent to 335 kcal.
  D The average western male is very vulnerable to obesity.

2 When we regulate our metabolism, we:
  A Cut down on food having a high fat content.
  B Take weight-reducing exercise on a daily basis.
  C Measure energy intake and output in percentage terms.
  D Balance food intake and exercise to keep body weight steady.

3 'Eating too much' is a 'facile' answer (l. 14) in that:
  (i) It does not explain everything that calls for explanation.
  (ii) It is too simple an answer to be taken seriously.
  (iii) This answer is true, but it is not the whole truth.
  (iv) There has to be a genetic basis for eating disorders.

  Answer:
  A if (i) and (iii) only are correct.
  B if (i), (ii) and (iii) are correct.
  C if (iv) only is correct.
  D if all are correct.

4 What shows that most obesity is non-genetic in origin?
  A It is hormones, not genes, that regulate energy balance.

Section 1

    B   Obesity has increased faster than possible gene pool mutation.
    C   We live a very sedentary life, and eat a high-fat diet.
    D   Changes in the gene pool occur over long time periods.

5 Obese people:
    A   Deceive experimenters because they are self-conscious.
    B   Overestimate the extent of their loss of body weight.
    C   Systematically understate the extent of their food intake.
    D   Eat less in normal life than when they are being tested.

Passage 2: Obesity: a weighty problem

6 Obese people get 'fat' because they:
    A   Eat too much carbohydrate-rich food.
    B   Have relatively large energy stores.
    C   Have an excess of triacylglycerol in adipose tissue.
    D   Suffer long-term changes in the body's energy stores.

7 Lean people on average:
    A   Have no difficulty controlling their energy intake.
    B   Tend to expend more energy than obese people.
    C   Do not store energy: output equals input.
    D   Have a lower food intake than obese people.

8 Studies of twins appear to indicate that:
    (i)   Approximately one third of BMI variability is genetic.
    (ii) Twins are particularly vulnerable to obesity problems.
    (iii) Genetic background is having an increasing influence.
    (iv) Non-genetic outweigh genetic factors in obesity.

    Answer:
    A   if (i) only is correct.
    B   if (i) and (iv) are correct.
    C   if (ii) and (iii) are correct.
    D   if all are correct.

9 Our genes appear to have an influence on obesity in that:
    A   They incline an individual to obesity or leanness.
    B   Energy expenditure is predetermined genetically.
    C   We have a genetic predisposition to eat or not to eat.
    D   They set limits to our individual energy requirements.

10 It is 'easier said than done' to counteract obesity in that:
    A   Obese people cannot resist eating energy-dense foods.
    B   There is more to obesity than regulating the energy balance.
    C   Eating less requires more will-power than obese people have.
    D   The stored part of obese people's energy balance is consistently positive.

Document response

Short-answer questions (Passages 1 and 2)

11 What do you think is meant by referring to the slimming industry as 'aggressive' (Passage 1, ll. 12–13)?

12 Passage 1 refers to 'our sedentary lifestyle' (l. 13 and l. 32). What illustrations of this lifestyle are given in Passage 2?

13 What are we to understand by 'metabolic causes of obesity' (Passage 1, l. 21)?

14 Passage 1 mentions 'psychological causes of obesity' (l. 23), and Passage 2 mentions 'psychological problems' (ll. 3–4). Are the two passages referring to the same things?

15 The two passages agree that most of the variability in BMI cannot be accounted for by our genes. Do they agree about the basis for our knowing this?

16 'In about a quarter of cases, obesity can be attributed to a person's genetic make-up' (Passage 1, ll. 25–26); 'about 30–40% of the variability in BMI is inherited' (Passage 2, l. 43). Are these two statements compatible?

17 Why need we not take the prediction that all Americans will be obese by 2230 too seriously (Passage 2, ll. 12–13)?

18 Do the two passages agree in their conclusions about what needs to be done to counteract obesity?

Essay question

'The proportion of adults who are overweight is rising sharply in developed countries.' Suggest what measures might be taken, by individuals and by society, to reverse the increase in obesity.

Answers

1 (b) The excess only has to be the equivalent of less than one chocolate bar daily. The references to Americans are incidental.

2 (d) We might do (a) and/or (b) in the process; we certainly do not need to do (c).

3 (a) It does not explain, for example, why certain people eat too much to the extent of self-harm — (i). The answer is true — as far as it goes — (iii).

4 (b) Obesity has increased too fast to be explained by a change in the gene pool. Both passages agree on this point. Answer (d) is true, but it is not an answer to this question.

5 (c) Answers (a) and (d) have a measure of truth about them — but the writer does not commit himself to an analysis of the subjects' motives.

Section 1

6 **(c)** The other forms of energy store do not cause long-term changes in body weight.

7 **(d)** Answers (a) and (b) may be true in individual cases; everybody stores energy — (c).

8 **(b)** It would appear that some 30–40% of the BMI variability can be attributed to our genes.

9 **(a)** They do not account for obesity but they 'control the tendency' to overeat or not to.

10 **(b)** There are complex psychological and other variables besides.

11 The slimming industry is 'aggressive' in that it bullies people into disliking their appearance, making them feel guilty, and thrusting 'remedies' at them.

12 Reference is made to children spending hours in front of a television or computer screen and to people in general using their cars rather than their feet.

13 These would be a malfunction of the organism, where the body would be physiologically unable to convert food energy to the body's use.

14 They are not referring to exactly the same things. Certain people may overeat as a result of depression or other neurotic state — these are 'psychological causes'. The psychological problems of Passage 2 are caused by growing social intolerance of obesity — obese people are made to feel ashamed.

15 They do. They both cite the speed at which obesity is increasing — a speed that far outstrips the speed of change in the gene pool.

16 They are compatible. The Passage 1 statement refers to a proportion of the population of obese people; the Passage 2 statement refers to the genetic/non-genetic variable in individual cases.

17 Such trends simply cannot continue. Public health and a rational distribution of food resources would not allow it. Besides, one cannot extrapolate from current data to circumstances more than 200 years hence.

18 Substantially they do agree: that we have to face the fact that social attitudes towards eating, and our current unhealthy lifestyle, must be taken in hand.

Essay question

We have two complementary positions here:

Position A	Position B
Measures that might be taken by individuals	Measures that might be taken by society

Each position will consist of a brief list of appropriate measures. They might as well be dealt with in the order suggested in the title — and as above. Any conclusion will probably be in the form of a summary of major points made.

Document response

It is plain that 'lifestyle' is the major cause of the massive increase in obesity in the western world. This has two components: the amount of what we eat and the circumstances in which we eat it; and what Prentice calls our 'modern sedentary lifestyle'. An individual can make changes on both fronts.

We have to accept that in certain patients eating disorders are the product of what might be called 'rogue genes' (or the interaction of rogue genes), or of psychological factors. Presumably there are limits to the autonomy — to the exercise of will-power — of an individual in the grip of psychosomatic depression or other neurotic condition. We can only concern ourselves here, therefore, with those individuals who are genuinely autonomous decision-makers.

It is unlikely that slimming remedies, as such, are the answer. Clearly, there are foods rich in polysaturated fats that are best avoided. But warnings against carbohydrates in the diet, which were common some years ago, were misguided. It cannot be stressed too often that it is a balanced diet that is to be desired. What frequently militates against this is the modern habit of 'grazing' — of eating snacks (crisps, biscuits and the like) and drinking sweet, canned drinks. Such casual eating is, perhaps, less easily controlled — the consumer monitors energy intake with less care — than in the context of regular meals at regular meal-times. In today's world, we say we do not have time for sit-down meals. Perhaps the truth is that we do not make time for such meals. This is a matter over which the individual could, it seems, reassume control.

On the other side of the energy balance equation, of course, is 'energy expenditure'. It is not necessary for an individual to enrol in a fitness club or make regular visits to a leisure centre to 'work out' in one or another ways, using more or less sophisticated equipment. What is necessary is that an individual makes a rational decision to walk, when his or her destination is within walking distance, rather than to drive; to go up the stairs to the office on the fourth floor rather than to use the lift; and to take the children out to the park to kick a football about rather than to buy them yet another computer game. Exercise is likely to be most effective for an individual when it is taken as a natural and everyday part of one's work-place and domestic life. Exercise that is taken as an adjunct to life — like weight-lifting or jogging — is not integral to it and can easily be discontinued; but exercise that is a complement to energy intake is likely to be sustained.

Just as it is in an individual's interest to keep healthy, so it is in society's interest to raise levels of public health — not least in order to reduce medical bills. More ambitiously, a healthy society is (potentially) a well-motivated, hard-working society. An obese society is one that is likely to be lethargic and unproductive — not to mention unhappy. A free society can hardly intervene in its citizens' eating habits; but it can require that manufacturers label their food products so that attention is drawn, for instance, to their sugar content. Limits may be set by legislation to the amount of such sugar content, if public opinion supported this move. Government is also in a position, in publicly maintained schools, to ensure that children eat healthy lunches

Section 1

and that fatty and sugary foods are not sold on school premises. Such controls could, in theory, extend to hospitals and all other public-sector institutions. Aside from such measures, a government can only issue information and advice.

Society is similarly limited in what it can do to foster a physically active citizenry. Again its remit may, in practical terms, be confined to the school system. At their most enlightened, PE and compulsory games command the participation of the majority of pupils — but they only provide a context for still more ridicule of the obese. Once again, physical activity — if it is to have the desired effects — must be pleasurable and be integrated into 'normal' activity, so that exercise is not perceived by the (potentially) obese as an unpleasant imposition that they discontinue at the earliest opportunity.

In the more public arena, society can provide suitable conditions for children to walk (or be walked) to school, and for more employees to take public transport to work — and thus walk for at least a part of the way. More roads could be pedestrianised, public paths could be made more attractive and more secure, and parking could be further restricted.

Perhaps in a society dedicated to growth and the 'good life', a minority of the self-indulgent is the price that we pay for freedom and consumerism. *(793 words)*

AO4 There is not much room for discussion here. The *facts* about obesity, and what could be done about it are increasingly well known. On the other hand, there is an issue of freedom here, and of human rights. This means we cannot be entirely *objective* about it. We can't be entirely objective about any issue involving humans, because we are human ourselves.

Section 2
Data response

Section 2

The 'application of number' is one of the 'key skills', the exercise of which is required on all General Studies papers.

In practice, the application of number is likely to mean the interpretation of statistical tables or diagrams. Tables will probably predominate, since these can incorporate a sizeable stock of figures. Of the graphical modes of representation, the most common are the line graph, the bar graph and the pie chart.

I have divided this section into the same three subject blocks as for Section 1, and have supplied:
- two 'arts' data sets (a line graph and a table);
- three 'social sciences' data sets (a table, a bar graph and a set of pie charts);
- two 'sciences' data sets (both of them tables).

On four out of the seven data sets I have set short-answer questions, and a short-essay question, calling for an answer of about 250–350 words. On each of the other three data sets I have set multiple-choice questions in addition.

If the tables or diagrams are effectively presented there should be no (generalisable) difficulty in interpreting them. What is required is a careful reading of names and labels, vertically and horizontally, and an observant eye for figures that are markedly larger or smaller than their neighbours. You will probably be asked to:
- identify trends in a line of figures;
- explain figures that are out of the ordinary;
- suggest reasons for discrepancies or equivalences;

and possibly:
- re-cast figures presented in one form into another: a table of percentages, say, as a pie chart or bar graph.

You may even have to do some sums, but they will not be more taxing than working out fractions or percentages, or converting one of these into the other. The worst thing would be for the (self-styled) non-mathematician to say 'I'm no good at maths', and to throw in the towel at the outset. The data sets with which you are presented will not have been culled from maths or science textbooks; they will have been taken from daily newspapers or weekly magazines. They will be information about social trends, for example, published by the government, in a quite easily digestible form. Or they will be the results of a social survey on a matter of some public importance and interest. They will not have been chosen for their abstruseness, or their power to mystify. The examiners themselves are highly unlikely to be hot-shot statisticians.

Section 2 Arts

Listening and viewing hours

The graph below shows the percentage of the British population that watches television, or that listens to the radio, at different times of the day.

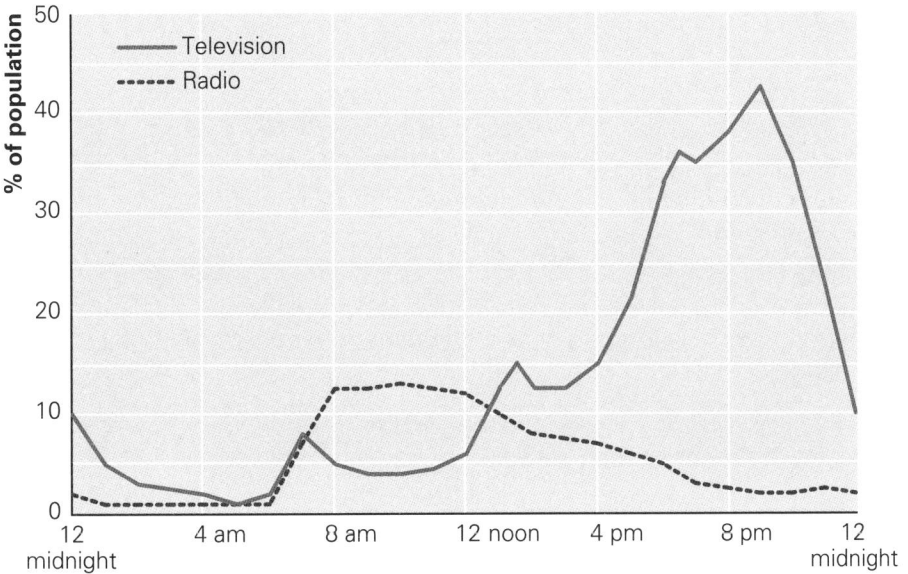

Short-answer questions

1 Between what times are more people listening to the radio than watching television?

2 Who do you think these listeners will be, and in what circumstances might they be listening?

3 What does the graph tell us about viewing and listening habits at breakfast time?

4 What can we deduce about viewing and listening habits at lunchtime?

5 Describe the television-viewing trend between 8 p.m. and midnight.

6 How do you account for this trend?

7 How do you account for the slight rise in listening to the radio between about 10 p.m. and 11 p.m.?

Section 2

8 To whom would such information as there is in the graph be of particular value, and why?

Short-essay question

The data in the graph represent listening and viewing figures for the population as a whole. Explain in what ways the habits of particular age groups may not conform to this pattern.

Answers

1. Between 7.15 a.m. and 12.30 p.m.

2. They may be drivers listening to their car radio on the way to work. Later in the morning they are probably housewives/husbands, or people who are housebound and have never adopted the habit of watching television in the morning — and who have other things to do.

3. TV viewing reaches a peak at 7.00 a.m. This is when people switch on to watch the news over an early breakfast, before going out to work. Radio listening starts a little later but goes on rising till 8.00 a.m. People can listen while eating, preparing to go out and driving.

4. Radio listening tails off after 12 noon, to be overtaken by TV watching at about 12.30 p.m. This rises to 15% at 1.30 p.m. — over lunch, perhaps.

5. Watching rises between 8 and 9 p.m., which is the so-called 'watershed'. Figures fall sharply between 9 p.m. (42.5%) and midnight (10%).

6. Children go to bed, progressively, after the watershed and viewing figures fall off generally as tiredness sets in, or as revellers go out (or as people prefer to watch a video or listen to music).

7. A small proportion of the population may return from an evening out and listen to the radio as they prepare for bed.

8. The information would be of particular use to:
   - advertisers who need to know when to buy broadcasting time so as to reach the maximum number of viewers and listeners;
   - programme planners who need to know when programmes are likely to achieve the highest ratings figures;
   - sociologists who make a study of people's leisure habits.

Short-essay question

The most obvious age groups that may not conform to the pattern presented in the graph are:
- young children;

Data response

- young people between the ages of 16 and 25;
- elderly people.

Identifying these groups is all you need to do by way of a plan. Allocate a short paragraph to each.

> Young children are unlikely ever to listen to the radio in preference to watching television. It is more difficult to concentrate on a disembodied voice than it is on moving images — and the latter are far more seductive. Very young children are unlikely to watch breakfast-time news programmes, but they may well form a majority of the 15% of the population watching at 1.30 p.m. They will also watch children's programmes in the afternoon.
>
> Adolescents and young adults watch television later in the evening, and into the early hours sometimes. They probably watch television rather than listen to the radio at breakfast time, but may have the radio on in their bedroom as they study, or get ready to go out.
>
> Elderly people are more likely to listen to the radio than watch television in the morning: they may not have got used to the fact that programmes are televised in the morning at all. They will be among the regular listeners to the *Today* programme, for instance, on Radio 4. Elderly people may well watch programmes like *Countdown* in the afternoon, but are less likely than younger people to watch much beyond 10 o'clock in the evening.
>
> Soap operas like *Coronation Street* and *EastEnders* achieve the high viewing figures that they do because they appeal to young and older adults alike. *(224 words)*

A04 Percentages are *facts*; but how we interpret these facts is partly speculative. I have drawn on the *soft evidence* of my own experience for the above interpretation.

Section 2 Arts

The world's most highly priced paintings

The following prices were paid at auction, up to 1 January 1995. Five further works by Picasso and four by Van Gogh reached prices exceeding £10 million.

Artist	Price (£ sterling)	Painting	Place	Date
Van Gogh	44,378,696	Portrait du Dr Gachet	New York	May 1990
Renoir	42,011,832	Au Moulin de la Galette	New York	May 1990
Picasso	33,123,028	Les Noces de Pierrette	Paris	November 1989
Cézanne	16,993,464	Nature Morte — les grosses Pommes	New York	May 1993
Manet	15,483,872	La Rue Mosnier aux drapeaux	New York	November 1989
Gauguin	13,496,934	Mata Mua, in olden times	New York	May 1989
Monet	13,000,000	Dans la Prairie	London	June 1988
Kooning	11,898,735	Interchange	New York	May 1990
Kandinsky	11,242,604	Fugue	New York	May 1990
Constable	9,800,000	The Lock	London	November 1990
Canaletto	9,200,000	Old Horse Guards, London from St James' Park with figures parading	London	April 1992
Matisse	8,741,723	Harmonie Fauve	New York	November 1992
Toulouse-Lautrec	6,982,249	Fille a la fourrure, Mademoiselle Jeanne Fontaine	New York	May 1990
Titian	6,800,000	Venus and Adonis	London	December 1991
Turner	6,700,000	Seascape, Folkestone	London	July 1984
Rembrandt	6,600,000	Portrait of a girl wearing a gold-trimmed cloak	London	December 1986
Goya	4,500,000	Bullfight: Suerte de Vares	London	December 1992
Leonardo da Vinci	3,364,879	Etude de draperie: personnage agenouillé, tourné vers la gauche	Monaco	December 1989
Rubens	3,000,000	Forest at dawn with deer hunt	London	December 1989
Velasquez	2,310,000	Portrait of Juan de Pareja	London	November 1970
Warhol	2,251,656	Marilyn	New York	November 1992

Data response

Multiple-choice questions

1 Gauguin's painting is of:
  A A village in provincial France.
  B New York when it was called New Amsterdam.
  C A scene from the Pacific island of Tahiti.
  D An ancient monument in Central America.

2 The painting by Leonardo da Vinci is of:
  A A clothed, kneeling figure.
  B A nude facing towards the left.
  C Drapery on a reclining figure.
  D A left-wing student of fashion.

3 *Marilyn*, Warhol's work, is a:
  A Painting in oils.
  B Screen print.
  C Montage of photographs.
  D Series of pen-and-ink drawings.

4 Rubens was a:
  A Painter at the court of Charles II.
  B German from the Black Forest.
  C Citizen of the Low Countries.
  D Favourite of Queen Victoria of England.

5 Turner painted:
  A Mostly portraits of aristocrats.
  B Tranquil British landscapes.
  C Pictures of nymphs and satyrs.
  D Storm-tossed visionary scenes.

Short-answer questions

6 What do the highest-priced paintings appear to have in common?

7 What is the ratio of the lowest-priced painting to the highest-priced painting of those sold in New York in May 1990?

8 What sort of paintings appear to sell in New York auction rooms?

9 What sort of paintings tend to come up for auction in London?

10 Why do you suppose works by Van Gogh, in particular, are valued so highly?

11 What is the mean price of those paintings in the table that were sold in London?

Section 2

12 Why do you think so many paintings fetched such high prices between 1989 and 1992?

Short-essay question

'The price of a painting and the value of a painting are two quite different things.' Discuss.

Answers

1 **(c)** Gauguin lived in Tahiti during his mature years, and it is the subject of all his best-known paintings.

2 **(a)** It is a study of a robe draped on a kneeling (*agenouillé*, from *genou*, meaning 'knee' in French) figure turned towards the left.

3 **(b)** Andy Warhol's 'Factory' is best known for its screen prints of Marilyn Monroe, of Coca-Cola bottles, and of Campbell's soup cans.

4 **(c)** Peter Paul Rubens, 1577–1640, lived for much of his life in Antwerp.

5 **(d)** Particularly famous are his Fighting Téméraire, his Rain, Steam and Speed and The Slave Ship.

6 The highest-priced paintings are all by impressionist, post-impressionist or cubist painters, working towards the end of the nineteenth and the beginning of the twentieth century.

7 The ratio is 1:6.356 (44,378,696/6,982,249 = 6.35593)

8 The New York auction rooms appear to make a speciality of highly priced and highly prized 'modern' works; the monetary value of such work is still capable of rising.

9 Paintings put up for auction in London tend to be British (Turner, Constable), of Britain (Canaletto), or old masters (Titian, Rembrandt). The Monet is an exception.

10 Van Gogh's style is distinctive: 'realistic', yet expressive of his personal angst. Public knowledge of the facts of his life lend poignant interest to his work.

11 £6,878,888.80 (61,910,000/9)

12 This was a period of economic boom, when there was a lot of 'hot' money about — particularly Japanese money from Tokyo property sales — chasing investment opportunities.

Short-essay question

There are two obviously conflicting positions here:

Position A	Position B
Price and value are highly correlated.	The price of a painting has nothing to do with its value (or vice versa).

Data response

You will need to refer to particular paintings and painters — but you will not need to refer to any not included in the table on p. 70. I will adopt the two positions in the above order, since my conclusion will approximate to Position B.

> What must be borne in mind is that a painting is the direct product of the artist's hand and imagination. Turner executed *Seascape, Folkestone* himself; the painting bears the impress of Turner's own skilled working. A painting is not like the first edition of a novel, or a building, or even the manuscript of a piece of music. It is truly a 'one-off'. It has a uniqueness — and therefore an intrinsic value — that no other work of art has. Turner, Rembrandt, Canaletto, Constable, Goya — each has been recognised for his genius as a draughtsman, and as a master of technical skills that defy imitation. Their works would be valued in any society, in any age.
>
> The same cannot, perhaps, be said of the work of many twentieth-century artists. To a certain extent this has been subject to the whim of fashion. Picasso, for example, is credited with having 'invented' cubism in 1905 (with his *Demoiselles d'Avignon*); and his giant *Guernica* is recognised for the masterpiece of stylised rage that it is. But no one would pretend that all his geometric faces and guitars are of equal value. There is something automatic about many of them — but if they bear the distinctive signature they fetch a distinctive price. The works of de Kooning and Kandinsky, similarly, are less obviously inherently 'skilful', or 'craftsmanlike', than the works of the old masters; but they have made their mark on twentieth-century art history in such a way as to suggest to investors that their names will not be forgotten.
>
> It is Warhol's *Marilyn*, however, that is the clearest example of the divorce of price from value. A screen print is essentially mass-produced: its 'value' is in its reproducibility. How can any one example, or sheet of examples, be 'worth' two and a quarter million pounds? The price acknowledges that the print was not, in fact, run off in multiples; but above all it reflects the extent to which Warhol immortalised certain icons of mid-twentieth-century culture, and the nature of his break with the fine-art tradition of 'unique' works of art.   *(346 words)*

AO4 *Value* is very much an AO4 word. Here it bears two senses: money-value and the (extrinsic) critical value that we place on a work of art. We can be *objective* about prices, but not about values in the second sense.

Section 2 *Social Sciences*

The family in Britain

The table below represents types of household in Britain, as percentages of the total, for the census years 1971, 1981, 1991 and 2001. (Note that the figures do not add up to 100 in all four columns because decimal figures have been rounded up or down to the nearest whole number.)

Households by type (percentages)	1971	1981	1991	2001
One-person households — over 65	6	8	11	15
One-person households — under 65	12	14	16	14
Two or more unrelated adults	4	5	3	3
One-family households:				
• married couple, no children	27	26	28	29
• one or two dependent children	26	25	20	19
• three or more dependent children	9	6	5	4
• non-dependent children only	8	8	8	6
Lone parent with dependent children	3	5	6	6
Lone parent with non-dependent children only	4	4	4	3
Two or more families	1	1	1	1
Total number of households (millions)	**18.6**	**20.2**	**22.4**	**24.1**

Short-answer questions

1 What can we deduce from the figures for one-person households over 65?

2 What can we deduce from the figures for one-person households under 65?

3 Is there anything to be inferred from the figures for married couples with no children?

4 What conclusions might we come to about the trends where the number of children per household is concerned?

5 What proportion of the total was accounted for by one-person households, in 2001?

6 How do we account for the trend in respect of lone parents with dependent children?

7 What was the percentage rise in the number of households between 1971 and 2001?

8 To what might we attribute the rise in the number of households over the period?

Data response

Short-essay question

Express a view as to some of the likely consequences for society if the trends represented in the table continue into the future.

Answers

1 The percentage has more than doubled, suggesting that people are living longer, or (what is more likely) that there are more single (divorced/widowed?) people who remain in, or settle into, a home of their own.

2 The figure for under-65s has remained rather stable. More people are choosing to remain single or more people are living separately from one-time partners, than in 1971, but fewer than in 1991.

3 The figure for childless couples has remained quite steady over the 30-year period. What the table does not show is whether couples are starting families later.

4 There is a drop of 12% in the proportion of married couples having children. The drop would seem to be accounted for by more people not marrying than by more married couples remaining childless.

5 29% (15+14)

6 The doubling of the percentage of lone parents is presumably accounted for by the rise in the number of separations and divorces, and by (generally) women who choose not to marry or live with their children's father(s).

7 29.57% (24.1 − 18.6 = 5.5; (5.5/18.6) × 100 = 29.57)

8 There is unlikely to have been a proportionate rise in the UK population overall in these years. The more likely explanation for the rise is the more than doubling of the percentage of one-person households, by a process of division.

Short-essay question

The trends are:
- more people living alone;
- fewer children;
- more lone parents.

The two likely consequences of these trends are:
- a declining overall population;
- the need for more housing units.

Whether there will be more, or less, 'happiness'/sense of fulfilment as a result of these trends is a more open question.

Section 2

> The population of Britain is more or less stable at present: there is a rough balance between deaths and births. People are perhaps living longer and healthier lives; but if the drop in the number of families with children continues, clearly the age profile of the population will rise (as, indeed, it is already doing), and overall population figures will decline. In a country that is already quite densely populated — particularly in the south-east — this may be no bad thing. We shall probably have less need for a sizeable labour market than in the past.
>
> More people are choosing to delay marriage, to terminate marriages or not to marry at all. The larger number of single-person households that there are, in consequence, will mean a greater future need for small housing units: small houses, and flats. This need has already been felt; and many local councils are having to allocate green-field sites to new building — especially in the south-western counties, and rural counties such as Cambridge and North Yorkshire, where there are few brown-field sites. The environmental consequences of all this new building will be significant.
>
> There is some evidence for the view that people who marry and have children suffer fewer mental health problems than those who live alone either by choice or by necessity. It may be that we are more fulfilled when we 'realise' our potential as partners and parents; and it goes without saying that separation and divorce are more likely to cause distress than delight, for all parties. If present trends continue into the future, therefore, we may be storing up problems for ourselves to which it is unlikely that there will be easy answers.
>
> *(280 words)*

AO4 There is a large measure of *subjectivity* here – but the final paragraph is based on some quite *hard evidence*. Family values are a topic to which one cannot help bringing a certain political *bias*.

Section 2 Social Sciences

The ageing process

The 'bars' in a bar graph may be set vertically or horizontally. In the graph below they are set horizontally. They represent the extent of self-reported health problems in the UK by gender and age for the year 1996–97.

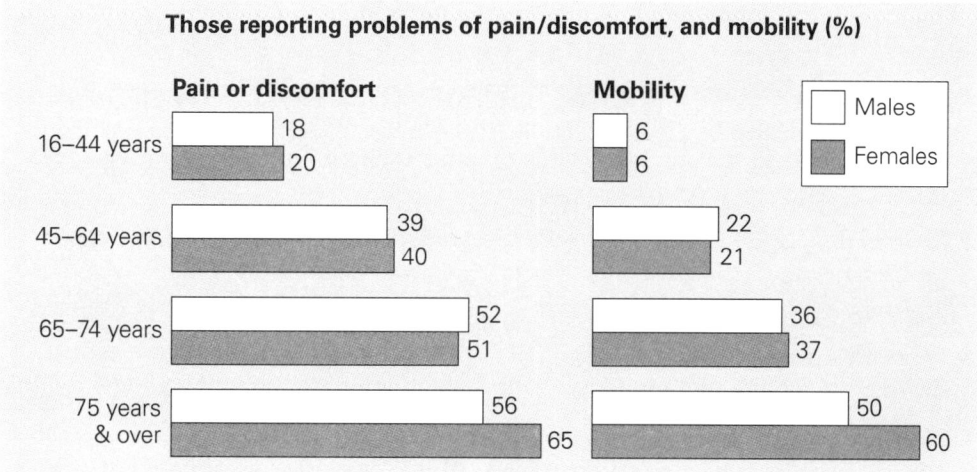

Short-answer questions

1 These are 'self-reported' health problems. To what extent should we treat them with caution?

2 What might be some of the causes of 'pain or discomfort' among males of 16–44 years?

3 Why might the pain or discomfort experienced by females in the 16–44 age group have different origins?

4 Why might it be difficult to make valid comparisons between one set of people and another in respect of the pain and discomfort that they experience?

5 Why might it be difficult to make comparisons between people in respect of their mobility?

6 What is the mean proportion of the total population reporting pain and discomfort?

7 Why do you suppose the differences between male and female percentages increase to such an extent in the '75 years and over' age group?

Section 2

8 Why do you think the percentages are consistently higher on the 'Pain or discomfort' side than on the 'Mobility problems' side of the graph?

Short-essay question

What steps might individuals take to delay, or mitigate, the effects of the ageing process?

Answers

1 When asked about their health by someone apparently sympathetic, many people will respond by 'opening up' self-pityingly — particularly if they are hopeful of a remedy. Some people are hypochondriacs; others are more stoical — or perhaps merely more reticent — about their aches and pains.

2 Males in this age group may suffer from sports injuries, or from the results of bravado. They may also experience the after-effects of occupational (manual) injuries, or motor accidents.

3 Women are subject to the afflictions of menstruation and childbirth that men are spared.

4 In addition to the hypochondria/stoicism problem mentioned above, there is the problem of definition: when is a slight ache a 'pain'? When is a 'discomfort' not worth mentioning? Different people have different pain thresholds.

5 Again, different respondents will have different views as to their mobility. Some people are rendered 'immobile', in their own opinion, by being deprived of their driving licence.

6 42.65% (18 + 20 + 39 ...+65)/8 = 42.625

7 Women have a longer average life span than men (80 years as against 75), therefore there will be larger numbers of elderly women than men in the population, of an age to report health problems.

8 'Pain or discomfort' is a category of problem more open to interpretation than 'mobility problems'. One may be afflicted by pain or discomfort in any one of a large number of limbs and organs. 'Mobility' is a more objectively understood notion.

Short-essay question

This is very much a list question: your answer will take the form of a number of 'steps'. These need not be arranged in any particular order.

The steps I shall suggest will concern:
- diet;
- exercise;
- posture and ergonomic furniture;
- attitudes and relationships.

This is probably as logical an order as any.

Data response

Nobody can delay the ageing process itself, of course; but there are 'lifestyle' steps that can be taken to stay healthy for longer, and so to mitigate the effects of ageing.

Amongst the most obvious measures are those that concern diet and exercise. These are interlinked, but let us look at diet first. It is a commonplace of practical-health literature that one should reduce the intake of fats and refined sugars to a minimum, in favour of fruit and vegetables. Unfortunately the signs are, still, that people in the lower income bracket eat more sugar and starchy foods, and far less fruit and vegetables, than people in the upper income bracket. Healthy eating continues to be associated with social-economic factors, whether out of ignorance, poverty or both. It may be added in this connection that heavy smoking and drinking will place strains on the system that may well lead to 'pain and discomfort' in later life.

It is not necessary to take exercise of a self-punishing sort, but regular walking and some physical effort ought to be a part of everyone's routine. Many spend a lot of time sitting down: such people should ensure that the chairs that they occupy are so designed as to enable them to sit comfortably and without strain. We also spend up to a third of our lives in bed, so it is important that our beds be not too soft and yielding.

It may seem that our attitudes and our relationships with others will have little bearing on our health and fitness: but those who live at ease with others will probably be those most at ease with themselves. There is an observed correlation between stability of mind and homeostasis of body. Mind and body are, after all, facets of the one psychosomatic system. It may be that optimism is a hereditary trait — that there is a gene for it — and that there is little that we can do to alter a natural predisposition to 'look on the black side'; but we owe it to ourselves and to others to cultivate habits of positive thinking. They do say, after all, that age is a state of mind.

(363 words)

> **A04** *Opinion* that is expressed here is quite firmly based on *facts* – so it cannot be dismissed as 'mere' opinion. There may be something *partial* about the diagnosis, though; I am probably a lot older than you are.

Section 2 Social Sciences

Economic status by gender and ethnicity

The following pie charts represent the employment patterns of men and women, and of different ethnic groups, in Great Britain. The numbers are percentages of the totals in each case.

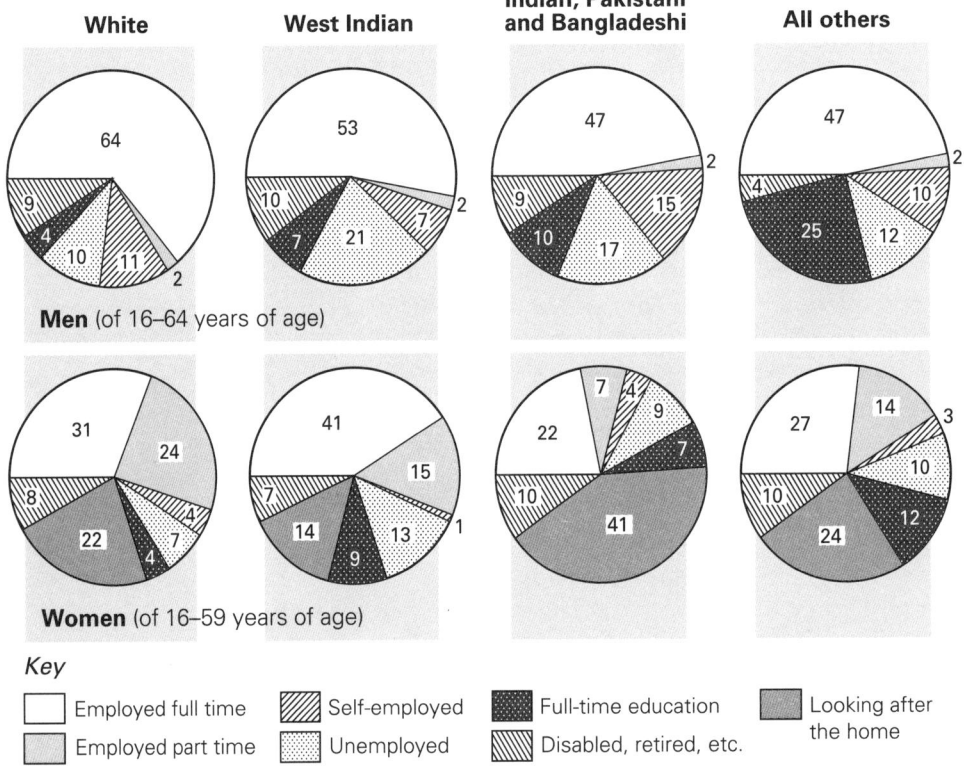

Multiple-choice questions

1 There is a higher percentage of West Indian than white males in full-time education because:
   A   More West Indians stay on to do A-levels and go to university.
   B   The ratio of young to adult West Indians is greater than in the white population.
   C   There are more West Indians of school age in the general population than there are whites.
   D   Schooling is more important in the West Indian than in the host culture.

Data response

2 Only 2% of all males work part time because:
  A There are very few part-time jobs to be had.
  B Women are more successful at acquiring such jobs than men.
  C Employers are prejudiced against employing male part-timers.
  D Men are the traditional breadwinners and need a full-time income.

3 We can account for the low percentage of disabled and retired males in the 'All others' chart by the fact that:
  A The Chinese and other Asians are relatively healthy.
  B These groups tend to retire much later, if at all.
  C This is a relatively young ethnic group, or groups.
  D These groups tend not to claim benefits or pension payments.

4 Indian, Pakistani and Bangladeshi women are least likely to take up employment because:
  A It is not part of their culture to go out to work.
  B Their husbands are harder-working than other male groups.
  C These women are most likely to be working for their husbands.
  D They are not protected by British equal-opportunities laws.

5 More than twice as many West Indian males are unemployed as white males. This may be because:
  A More West Indians than whites are disabled or retired.
  B Wage labour is not a part of West Indian culture.
  C West Indian males are contemptuous of 'white' qualifications.
  D There is still prejudice against employing blacks among some employers.

Short-answer questions

6 What is the mode proportion of disabled, retired people across all eight groups?

7 How might we account for the high proportion of males from the Indian subcontinent who are self-employed?

8 What is the ratio of whites to West Indians in full-time education?

9 Why do you suppose a smaller proportion of West Indian females stay at home than other female groups?

10 What do you infer from the fact that a higher proportion of West Indian males (53%) are in full-time employment than males in other non-white groups (47%)?

11 How do you account for the fact that white women are least likely to be registered unemployed?

Section 2

12 Why do you think there are higher proportions of boys than girls in full-time education among non-white, non-West Indian groups?

Short-essay question

The data in the pie charts represent the situation in the present (or recent past). Suggest what might be some likely trends in the future.

Answers

1 **(b)** The age profile of the West Indian population is lower than among whites, so there is a higher ratio of young West Indians to adults than among whites.

2 **(d)** Men in all ethnic groups have traditionally 'brought home the bacon'. This has generally meant that they needed to be in full-time employment, in order to earn a 'living' wage.

3 **(c)** This is a group, or groups, with a relatively young age profile — and is witness to by the fact that 25% of them (Hong Kong Chinese, Singaporeans, Malays, etc.) are in full-time education.

4 **(a)** Most of these women will have joined husbands working in Britain. Many of them will be Muslim and therefore will not be expected to work outside the home.

5 **(d)** In addition, black youths may not be (or be seen to be) well disposed to playing by white rules.

6 10%. The mode is the most frequent proportion. In three of the pie-charts the proportion of disabled, retired people is 10%.

7 These men might well have run small (often retail) businesses in their home countries. This, therefore, was the sort of work they took up in Britain — notably newsagents and small grocery stores.

8 1:2. The proportion is 4 for white men and women, and 8 (the mean of 7 and 9) for West Indian men and women.

9 There is no cultural bias against West Indian women being employed. They may have to be the breadwinners when their husbands cannot find work. Many probably work out of economic necessity.

10 There is less of a tradition of self-employment among West Indians than among other ethnic groups; and a smaller proportion of West Indians of 18+ are likely to be in higher education than among Asian groups.

11 A white 'housewife' may not think of herself as unemployed. Her husband is, of all male groups, most likely to be in full-time employment, therefore she will not be actively seeking work — especially if she has younger children.

12 There is still a strong tradition of boys being given more educational opportunities than

Data response

girls among these groups. Boys are more likely to travel to British institutions on their own than girls.

Short-essay question

One trend has been mentioned in the answer to question 7 above: males looking after the home.

Other possible trends are:
- a growth in the proportion of those who are retired;
- growth in proportions of those in full-time education;
- growth in the self-employment category.

Each of these trends is worth a brief paragraph of its own.

Staying on at school or going to college at the age of 16 is likely to become the norm, as in America. There will be fewer 16–18-year-olds in full-time employment. The proportion of 18/19-year-olds going on to degree-awarding institutions is likely to grow, too, as higher-level qualifications come to be necessary in more and more employment sectors.

It is possible that full-time workforces, and employment opportunities, will shrink. Employment will be increasingly casualised. This, in turn, will mean that more and more employees will work part time, and that more and more people will work on a freelance basis, perhaps from home, in IT-related fields.

A feature of working life in the 1990s was the trend towards taking retirement early — and significantly earlier than the 'retirement age' of 65 for men and 60 for women. This trend was a product of company 'downsizing' and the shake-out of middle-management professionals in business, teaching and other sectors. This trend is likely to continue, in association with the trend towards self-employment and looser full-time employment structures.

As more women have entered the labour force, so distinctions between 'men's work' and 'women's work' have been eroded. The institution of marriage also imposes fewer conventions on couples than in the past. As a result, it is less 'odd' than it used to be for a wife and mother to work, and for a husband to stay at home and look after the house and children. As more people work from home, the notion of the workplace will continue to be blurred — as, perhaps, will be the notions of 'work' and 'employment' themselves.

(270 words)

AO4 Perhaps any exercise in futurology is bound to be AO4 in that, whilst *hard evidence* is the launch pad, one is taking off into the thinning air of *opinion*, and *partiality*. What is important is that one is aware of this.

Section 2 Sciences

Infectious diseases

The following are World Health Organisation (WHO) figures for the populations affected by various infectious diseases in the mid-1990s.

Disease	Incidence	Deaths
Acute respiratory infections	248 million	4.1 million
Bacterial meningitis	1.2 million	210,000
Cholera	380,000	6,800
Dengue/DHF	560,000	23,000
Diarrhoeal diseases	1.8 billion	3 million
Hepatitis B	2.2 million	1 million
HIV/AIDS	2–3 million	700,000
Japanese encephalitis	40,000	11,000
Leishmaniasis	7.2 million	197,000
Malaria	300–500 million	2 million
Measles	45 million	1.2 million
Polio	110,000	5,500
Schistosomiasis	200 million	200,000
Tuberculosis	8.8 million	2.7 million
Whooping cough	4.3 million	360,000
Yellow fever	200,000	30,000

Short-answer questions

1 What is an infectious disease?

2 Which appears to be the most widespread of these diseases?

3 To what extent might it be said that diarrhoeal diseases are less serious than, say, hepatitis B or tuberculosis?

4 Why do you suppose there is so much uncertainty about the incidence of malaria?

5 Which disease, once contracted, is most likely to prove fatal?

6 What is the statistical chance of dying once one has contracted schistosomiasis?

Data response

7 What proportion of tuberculosis patients die from the disease?

8 Of all the diseases referred to, which appear(s) to have been most effectively brought under control? Why do you think this is?

Short-essay question

'All the really serious diseases afflict the poor world, yet all the serious money is spent fighting the diseases of the rich world.' Discuss.

Answers

1 An infectious disease is one that can be caught by exposure to harmful bacteria.

2 The most widespread (and second most fatal in absolute terms) diseases are diarrhoeal. These afflict 1.8 billion people world-wide.

3 Considering how widespread they are, diarrhoeal diseases result in relatively fewer deaths than other diseases (i.e. a smaller proportion of those subject to these diseases die from them). They are serious, of course, in virtue of their being so common.

4 Malaria is almost endemic in certain regions. Its incidence may well not be notified to the authorities, and it is not always likely to be fatal.

5 Hepatitis B: nearly one half of cases (one in every 2.2) proves to be fatal.

6 The chance of dying is one in a thousand.

7 The proportion is 30.68% $(2.7/8.8) \times 100$.

8 Cholera and polio have been brought under fairly effective control: the former because of improved sanitary facilities for more of the world's population; and the latter because of a sustained immunisation programme.

Short-essay question

There is enough truth in the statement to make it a matter of debate. The two positions that might be taken up are, of course:

Position A	**Position B**
A huge amount of research money is spent in the West on e.g. a cure for cancer.	What is needed in the poor world, often, is access to fresh water.

It is difficult to agree wholeheartedly with the quotation because it is an over-simplification ('All ... all ...'). But I shall go some way towards it.

When people inflict diseases on themselves — by smoking and contracting lung cancer; by engaging in unprotected, promiscuous sex and catching AIDS; or by overeating and dying of heart failure — it is not easy to defend large expenditures on seeking cures for these conditions. Many cancers and inherited diseases, however, are not the product of ill-advised behaviour. Where there is a good chance that research expenditure might yield effective treatments for these diseases, the money is well spent. In this connection, it must be borne in mind that AIDS afflicts African countries far more severely than countries in the 'western world' — so it may be hoped that remedies for the disease might have a very widespread application.

To be sure, the same sums of money could be spent alleviating poverty, lack of hygiene, and parasitic and insect-borne disease in the poor world. Here people die of easily treated illnesses before they reach an age when they might be subject to one or another malignant cancer. But who would pay the vast sums needed to combat the diseases of poverty and ignorance? The drug companies conduct much of their research in the rich world, because they look for an economic return on investment. As things are, they could hardly be expected to behave like aid organisations. The single most effective remedy against disease in the poor world would be access to fresh water. To supply this would require a huge international effort calling for decisions and actions of a political kind.

We know how to combat many of the killer diseases, especially hunger and dehydration. Of course, 'serious money' is needed — but it is unlikely to be the same serious money as that which is spent on legitimate medical research wherever this takes place. Besides, the money spent on this research will benefit humanity as a whole in the long term. Meanwhile, what is needed is an act of international political goodwill.

(320 words)

A04 Any 'political' issue has a *values* element. I attach a lot of value to measures to alleviate LDC poverty, so I broadly agree with the quotation in the question. I am not impartial.

Section 2 Sciences

Carbon emissions

The following table shows carbon emissions from the burning of fossil fuels, by the twenty countries most responsible for emissions in 1994.

Country	Emissions per person (tons)	Emissions per $GNP (tons per million $)	Total emissions (million tons)	Emissions growth 1990–94 (%)
Australia	4.19	230	75	4.2
Brazil	0.39	70	60	15.8
Canada	3.97	200	116	5.3
China	0.71	330	835	13.0
France	1.56	80	90	–3.2
Germany	2.89	140	234	–9.9
India	0.24	160	222	23.5
Iran	1.09	270	62	n/a
Italy	1.81	110	104	0.8
Japan	2.39	110	299	0.1
Kazakhstan	4.71	1,250	81	n/a
Mexico	0.96	140	88	7.1
North Korea	2.90	960	67	n/a
Poland	2.31	460	89	–4.5
Russia	3.08	590	455	–24.1
South Africa	2.07	680	85	9.1
South Korea	1.98	200	88	43.7
UK	2.62	150	153	–0.3
Ukraine	2.43	60	125	–43.5
USA	5.26	210	1,371	4.4

Multiple-choice questions

1 'Fossil fuels' will include:
  A Coal, oil, gas and hydroelectricity.
  B Nuclear fuel, coal and oil, but not natural gas.
  C All non-renewable fuels except natural gas.
  D Wood, coal, oil and gas, but not nuclear fuel.

Section 2

2 What might 'n/a' in the 'Emissions growth' column indicate?
  A Figures for earlier years are unavailable.
  B These countries have only recently started burning fossil fuels.
  C The figures are too low to be statistically significant.
  D These countries refuse to divulge growth figures.

3 Which country would seem to contribute most to global warming?
  A South Korea.
  B The USA.
  C India.
  D Kazakhstan.

4 What can be said about the four countries with the highest growth rates?
  A They are enjoying rapid economic development.
  B They are countries that are fast slipping into poverty.
  C People use fuel extravagantly in these countries.
  D These countries have no alternative sources of energy.

5 Ukraine is likely to have reduced emissions over the period because:
  A A stringent conservation policy has been in force.
  B The country has switched from fossil fuels to renewables.
  C The economy has suffered a marked slowing down.
  D Since Chernobyl, Ukraine has shut down its reactors.

Short-answer questions

6 What is the mean figure for emissions for EU nations in the table?

7 What do you think accounts for the high emissions per person in the USA?

8 How does India come to have the lowest figure for emissions per person, yet the second highest growth rate over the period?

9 How do you account for the high figures for emissions in Kazakhstan?

10 Why might Germany's emissions have fallen by 10% over the 4-year period?

11 How do the figures for South Korea compare with those for Mexico?

12 What does the high figure for North Korea in the 'Emissions per dollar GNP' column tell us about this country?

Short-essay question

What do these figures suggest might be the most appropriate policies for combating global warming?

Data response

Answers

1 **(d)** A fossil fuel is the product of biological decomposition; nuclear fuel — uranium — is a naturally occurring element. Of course, in theory it is a finite resource, and therefore non-renewable.

2 **(a)** Iran and North Korea were secretive countries, likely to be suspicious of western data gatherers. Kazakhstan was still in some turmoil following the breakup of the Soviet Union. (It is, perhaps, remarkable that figures in the other three columns were available from these countries in 1994.)

3 **(b)** The USA carbon emissions are highest (by far) in terms of the annual total, and in terms of per capita tonnage. And emissions were still growing in 1994.

4 **(a)** They are enjoying rapid economic development — or they were, in the period under review. All started from a relatively low base. South Korea was one of the Asian 'tigers' whose economy — and therefore car use and industrial plant construction — boomed. India, China and Brazil experienced growth overall, though individual Indians and Chinese would scarcely have noticed.

5 **(c)** Ukraine was a victim of the sudden end of the Soviet empire, and of the turbulence in the once assured market for its products.

6 2.22 tons per person (this is the mean of the figures for Germany, France, Italy, and the UK).

7 The USA is a highly motorised country — so much of the tonnage will be emissions from 'gas-guzzling' cars. But the USA also suffers from extremes of heat and cold, so air-conditioning and central heating will be significant contributors.

8 India has a very big population. Individuals use little fuel; but a billion individuals — each gradually using a little more — use a lot. India has been industrialising throughout the 1990s, so emissions will continue to climb.

9 It is a cold country in winter, a sparsely populated country and a poor country. Its population will heat and cook with fossil fuels — and heating oil accounts for a higher proportion of (a very low) GNP than anywhere else. Total emissions, though, are relatively low.

10 Germany will have switched from coal burning in these years, particularly the ex-communist east (the old GDR). Pollution will have been reduced in the east as inefficient industries closed down.

11 Both countries produce the same tonnage of carbon emissions, i.e. 88m. Each Mexican produces only half what each South Korean produces, however; and South Korea has enjoyed much faster economic growth than Mexico — hence a six-times-bigger emissions growth rate.

12 Like Kazakhstan, North Korea is a poor country, and a cold one in winter. Its GNP is very low, therefore expenditure on fuel will be high as a proportion of all expenditure.

Section 2

Short-essay question

🖉 This is not really a question that can be answered in terms of two positions, A and B; the list approach would be better here. A number of policies might be suggested, one after another. These might include the following:

(a) To work to reduce emission per person in the highly industrialised countries.

(b) To undertake large-scale research and development of non-fossil alternative fuels.

(c) To assist China and India, in particular, to develop in environment-friendly ways.

I shall devote a short paragraph to each of these policies.

On the face of it, the USA is the real rogue: the average North American releases more carbon into the atmosphere than citizens of any other country; and because the population is large (something over 250 million) the total emissions are correspondingly large — yet cars are bigger than they need to be, speeds on interstate highways are rising, and petrol prices are the lowest (because tax is the lowest) of all the countries in the western world. The Australians and Canadians, it should be said, are profligate users of fossil fuels also; but because their populations are relatively small, total emissions for these countries are small in proportion. All three countries are wealthy enough to be setting a better example of responsible fuel use than they are presently doing. One clear policy, then, might be to persuade the US government to raise a tax on petrol that would pay for research into renewable fuels. No one country can duck its responsibilities for reducing harmful emissions.

Nuclear power promised relief from such harm, at one time; but it has threatened harm of other sorts. We owe it to our children to invest in sustainable ways of generating power. Wind, wave and solar power are all promising alternatives if only we were prepared to fund them. Big oil and motor manufacturing companies, as well as wealthy oil-producing states, have an interest in and a responsibility for ensuring that — as the oil runs out — there are other means at our disposal of powering industry and our cherished mobility.

India and China have as much right to industrialise as any countries in the 'developed' world. But if the industrialisation harnesses old technology, their contribution to global warming will multiply a hundredfold. Banks and transnational companies must be constrained to locate and invest in these countries on condition that they learn from mistakes made elsewhere. 'Where there's muck there's brass' cannot be the motto of the emerging economies — not, at least, where that muck is carbon. India must be assisted to harness its sunshine; China its wind. Global warming obliges us to think globally. *(349 words)*

AO4 Here again, my values are evident. Any catalogue of recommendations will be subjective in some measure. The above answer would have looked different if it had been written by a Texas oilman.

Section 3

Essays

Section 3

Once again, the section is divided into three blocks. I have chosen four essay titles in each block, of a sort that are the staple of General Studies papers.

First of all, I decide which of two sorts of essays the title seems to demand. I referred to these in my introduction to Section 1 as a 'two-positions' essay and a 'list' essay. An essay is often the argument of a case. There are always two possible points of view in any debate — and there are often several more; but two points of view, or positions, are all you need represent in the time you have at your disposal. The important thing is not to give the impression that you think there is only one.

Q **'A network of good open roads is vital to a country's economic growth.' Discuss.**

There are two obvious positions here. You will probably be more sympathetic to one of them than the other before you begin — so you will know what conclusion you will want to come to. Deal with the argument with which you disagree, briefly, first; then lay out your own argument, so as to be able to go straight on to the conclusion. This is how I would argue:

Position A
Roads are necessary, because they link centres of supply and demand. They give door-to-door access. They are paid for out of public money.

Position B
The centres are becoming increasingly congested. Heavy traffic is a source of pollution. Roads have already spoilt much of our environment. Users should bear the real costs.

I would then want to give one or two examples of insensitive road building, of congestion, and of alternatives to road building (more flexible rail communications, use of canals, the development of local 'farmers' markets' to cut food miles, road pricing, etc.)

My conclusion would then be that building more and more roads is unsustainable, particularly in view of the conclusive evidence adduced by Friends of the Earth that road building creates traffic.

A quotation (or quasi-quotation) presented for discussion is generally contentious. It is a classic device for presenting an argument for discussion that is considered wide open. You may agree with it or disagree with it: either way, you should:
- present both sides of the argument;
- give real-life examples, perhaps based on your own experience or reading, on both sides if possible, but at least on the side of the argument with which you agree. Come to a conclusion based on this example, or — preferably — these examples.

It is unlikely that you would need to clarify the meaning of this particular title before beginning, but you would probably make an opening statement of your intent. For example:

'I intend to present arguments in defence of this proposition and arguments that oppose it. I will conclude that, on balance, the arguments for alternatives to a never-ending road-building programme are stronger than for "a network of good open roads" that, in practice, is pure nostalgia.'

Your conclusion should then tally with this statement of intent. For example:

'I have argued that we shall never again have "good open roads" in densely populated countries like England and that, therefore, we should seek other ways of improving the transport of goods and people that is vital to economic growth.'

You might prefer to subvert the quotation altogether by arguing either that economic growth in the future is much more likely to be based on information flow and digital technology than on the transport of freight; or that economic growth is simply not a desirable — because ultimately it is not a sustainable — national (or international) objective.

Such a strategy carries less risk in General Studies than in many another subject; but you will still need to argue your case, and take 'mainstream' arguments seriously.

Q What alternatives to prison are there for minor offenders for whom a prison sentence would be unsuitable?

This is more likely to be a short-essay than a long-essay question: the essential point here is that the statement is intended to be uncontentious. You are expected to agree that a prison sentence would be 'unsuitable' for (unnamed and unnumbered) categories of 'minor offenders'. There is no reason why you should not briefly contend that prison is unsuitable for many not-so-minor, non-violent offences, as long as you do not delay your exploration of alternatives. With the same proviso, you could open your essay by giving reasons for the unsuitability of prison for minor offenders: the fact that they lose the job that is the best guarantee of future good conduct; that their family is punished as much as they are; that they meet more seasoned criminals than themselves, and so on.

This title invites you to write what is essentially a list of alternative measures — probation, a fine, community service, electronic tagging — explaining briefly what each involves and discussing the advantages and disadvantages of each. Your conclusion might well give support to any one of the alternatives that you have referred to, whether this is one in common use, or one that you have read about, or one that is your own.

Section 3 Arts

Architecture

Question

In what sense would you say that the character of our age is reflected in our architecture? Refer to one or more particular buildings in your answer.

It's as well to agree, broadly, with the thrust of the question here. After all, the age is multifaceted and so is modern architecture. So your answer will be in the form of a list of parallels, with an example of each:

1. characteristic of age ⟶ style of architecture ⟶ building
2. ditto ⟶ ditto ⟶ ditto
3. ditto ⟶ ditto ⟶ ditto

All you need say in your introduction is that age and architecture are both complex in character.

You could well assert in your conclusion that architecture is bound to reflect the character of the age: after all, architects and the people who brief them both live in the same age — so both will be influenced by salient features of their society, as well as of its technology.

Answer

The present age is complex. True, we all live in the same social market now. Capitalism has triumphed; companies are expanding in size and going global — but we are not all in business. Not surprisingly, our architecture is complex too. ◁ Introduction

Skyscrapers were built in New York to save space. Architects like Le Corbusier and Mies van de Rohe made a virtue of necessity: their towers were things of austere beauty. They set the tone for building after the Second World War. In the 1980s and 1990s there has been a third reason for building towers: corporate prestige — even national prestige. The Canary Wharf tower in London's redeveloped docklands is an example of the striving for height, almost for its own sake. It represented the thrusting entrepreneurialism of Mrs Thatcher's day — and it is significant that it is where Mr Blair chose to receive powerful European leaders for 'summit' talks. The Trump Tower is one American example of this trend; and the Twin Towers of Kuala Lumpur is another. These towers are demonstrations of what civil engineers can do almost more than architects.

◁ 1st characteristic: corporate confidence ⟶ towers

◁ 1st example

◁ 2nd and 3rd examples

Essays

High-rise buildings did not work for housing, however. The middle classes never had to live in them; they were essentially for 'social', or council housing. We aspire to be a classless society — even if we are far from being one in practice. We all, therefore, want to live in what are recognisably houses, having their own front door, a patch of garden, and — probably — a pitched roof. Flat roofs really didn't work; and nor did prefabricated concrete panels — they suffered from 'fatigue'. So modern housing tends to be built of brick, and to be roofed with tiles. Such housing is not very different from those houses in which the middle classes have always lived in this century, except that plastic window frames are standard, and there is no need of chimney stacks. No particular example of this new style of housing stands out. Wates, Berkeley and Fairclough 'homes' are to be found everywhere — and so are their social-housing imitators.

◀ 2nd characteristic: social-class mobility → traditional brick houses

Bright colours are a characteristic of a number of modern buildings, such as the Beaubourg in Paris and Lloyds of London. The blue and red piping exposed on the facades of these otherwise glass and metal structures express the zany flamboyance of our age — otherwise expressed in in-your-face pop music and 'fashion' shows. Novelty is a strong driving force in all the arts — and architecture is no exception: it is the eccentric structure that stands out — like Pei's glass pyramid at the Louvre, and the Arche de la Défense, also in Paris, and the Guggenheim gallery in Bilbao, Spain.

◀ Examples

◀ 3rd characteristic: colourful, eccentric buildings

There is a confidence about the present age; but there is a certain temporariness also. Buildings are not always built to last as they used to be. This is partly because of their experimental nature, and because of the materials with which they are made. The Dome at Greenwich is a well-known example of this trend. It harks back to the Dome of Discovery at the 1951 Festival of Britain, and its purpose is much the same: to be an exhibition space. It is striking to look at — but it has no architectural relationship with its surroundings; and it may well deteriorate in a quite short time. This is not what we generally expect from our major buildings — but it may be the pattern in the new millennium.

◀ More examples

◀ 4th characteristic: confidence, yet impermanence

◀ Example

Architecture is bound to reflect the character of the age; after all, architects, the people who brief them and the people who use the buildings all live in the same age and are influenced by it. Architecture is the art of enclosing space. That space has a certain specified use — and the character of the age, its activities and preoccupations, will be what defines the use to which buildings are to be put.

◀ Conclusion

🅔 The title is very much in the present tense ('... our age is reflected in our architecture'), so I wrote only about modern times and modern buildings. I think I would do the same again. It would hardly have been appropriate — other than in a brief introduction, perhaps — to refer to previous ages: to the religious spirit of the 'gothic' period; to the neo-classicism of the Augustan Age; or the fusion of new and old in Victorian 'gothick' buildings.

Still, the examples I have given are rather conventional. I could have referred to the new Hindu temple at Neasden, north London, the biggest outside the Indian subcontinent; or to the rebuilt Reichstag, in Berlin, as reflecting both a return to the past and a reinterpretation of that past.

AO4 There are a number of *opinions* expressed here. *Evidence* is supplied, however, in the form of examples of actual buildings – so the opinions do have *objective* support.

Section 3 Arts

The arts and public money

Question

A great deal of public money is spent, directly or indirectly, on the arts in Britain. Advance arguments for and against this expenditure.

> You will not need to know how much money is spent (who does know this?); but you will need to know something about how the money is allocated, and about what the money is spent on.

The main thrust of the question is whether such money should be spent or not. The essay should fall into two roughly equal halves; one half should consist of a short series of arguments one way, and the other half should consist of the arguments for the other:

Position A
Arguments for the spending of public money on the arts.

Position B
Arguments against such expenditure.

I shall reverse the order of these two sets of arguments in my answer, because I shall want to conclude that the expenditure is justified. It is open to you to come down on one side or the other.

Answer

Before the Second World War, private patrons commissioned works of art, and private theatre managers gave space to plays and shows that would turn a profit at the box office. Art was commissioned, produced and paid for by private individuals. The Arts Council was established by the Labour Government of 1945–50. It was the aim of this body to be a channel for public funds to those activities that were considered to contribute to the 'public good'.

⊲ A brief historical introduction. It sets out the background to the debate — but these points could as well have been made within the context of the two positions taken in this essay.

The work of the Arts Council went unquestioned during the period of the so-called 'Post-War Consensus' of 1945–79. Both major political parties thought of the arts as an extension of education — and few questioned that this was a state responsibility. A policy change took place after 1979 with Mrs Thatcher's accession to office as Prime Minister. It was her view, and the view of her governments, that the arts should pay their way, as

⊲ Position B: arguments against subsidising the arts from public moneys

commercial activities. If people wished to go to the theatre they would go: if it was a 'good' play it would command 'good' audiences who would pay to see it, and it would have a 'good' run and be profitable. Andrew Lloyd Webber's musicals did not need a public subsidy, because they were the sort of shows that people wanted to see. They were successful because they were 'good' — and no amount of public money would make a good show out of a bad one. Mrs Thatcher did not dismantle the Arts Council, but her government did set tighter limits to funding and encourage private and company sponsorship of what might have been awarded grants from the public purse before 1979.

Why should poets, painters, playwrights and musicians live off the state when other people had to make a living without assistance? Let the market decide, said the New Right; let theatre-goers and opera buffs pay for their pleasures at the going rate, and let others enjoy the money in their pocket that came with lower and lower levels of income tax.

◀ The 'market forces' argument

Conservative Party ideology (which, of course, had an impact across a range of public services and utilities) coincided with a 'tabloid' impatience of much 'modern' painting, theatre and music. Why should the public pay through taxation what it would not pay to watch or to listen to by choice? The arts, and the art establishment, seemed to have moved away from public taste as if it thought it could dictate it rather than reflect it. Why should the public pay artists to produce works at seemingly higher and higher levels of abstraction that often cocked a snook at decency and conventional values — or that were downright incomprehensible?

◀ Public taste and the remoteness of much modern art

It is no bad thing that there should be a connection between what people are prepared to pay for and what artists provide. On the other hand, it is argued, the market should not be allowed to impose its own values on artistic endeavour, to the exclusion of other social and moral values. We go on paying a licence fee so that the BBC can bring us national events and broadcast arts programmes that ought not to be at the whim of advertisers and managers fixated on audience ratings. In the same way, we should be prepared to provide out of public funds what the market might neglect: opera and ballet productions that lend the nation a certain prestige on the world stage; orchestras and theatre companies (like the Royal Shakespeare Company) that are expensive to maintain, but without which our cultural life would be very much poorer; and activities in the regions of Britain that

◀ Position A: arguments for some public funding of the arts

often complain, with justice, that they suffer neglect in comparison with provision in London.

With a little support and encouragement, artists and writers (no less than sportspeople) can be enabled to realise their potential, pay their way and benefit all of us. What is more, society needs to be challenged by its creative thinkers; television, the West End, the commercial cinema chains, left to themselves, will entertain us to death. There is more to life than *Coronation Street*, *The Mousetrap* and the *Star Wars* trilogy.

◀ The function of art to challenge and debunk

The public should not be expected to 'feather-bed' self-indulgent producers of what they — but not the public, and few critics — call 'art'; we are short neither of daubs nor of verses. But awarded selectively, on merit, public subsidies can help groups, companies, bands, galleries, orchestras, fill gaps in provision that the market would leave unfilled.

◀ Conclusion: a balancing of the positions — and a preference for that more recently expounded

I might have given more specific examples, perhaps: I could have referred to the Culture Secretary's welfare-to-work scheme, whereby struggling musicians could be paid to work in music shops and for recording companies. Equally, I could have referred to the commercial success of the work of the late Ted Hughes (*Birthday Letters*) and of the screenplay of our premier 'highbrow' dramatist, Tom Stoppard (*Shakespeare in Love*). But I would have come to the self-same compromise conclusion.

AO4 As in the context of 'The World's Most Highly-Prized Paintings' we have a clear (AO4) distinction here between *value* for money, and values of a different kind. There is a clear distinction, too, between, the public-service *ideology* of the Arts Council and the BBC, and the ideology of 'new right' economic liberalism.

Section 3 Arts

Censorship

Question

Anxiety is often expressed about material on the stage, on the screen and in the press that is in questionable taste. How far do you think the authorities are justified in censoring such material?

There are two or three sub-questions that it is worthwhile considering before tackling the main question about justification:
(a) What sort of material is it that is in questionable taste?
(b) Who are the 'authorities'?
(c) What do we mean by 'censoring'?

I shall try to answer each of these questions in turn — in the above order — before setting out arguments for each of the two positions:

Position A
Censorship is justified.

Position B
Censorship is not justified.

What conclusions I come to will probably depend upon the nature of the 'material' under review, and how broadly or narrowly I define 'censorship'. You will not be expected to be familiar with material in 'questionable taste', at first hand, to be eligible to answer this question, so you may have rather few examples at your disposal.

Answer

For material to be thought of as lacking in taste, it must challenge commonly accepted standards of behaviour. Violence is not usually thought of as a matter of taste (few consent to violence being done to them, therefore it is a moral matter). So I shall not consider media violence in this essay. When we talk of taste, we generally refer to what is allegedly pornographic, or concerns bodily functions other than the reproductive; and the satirical treatment of persons or institutions that borders on ridicule. Material is said to lack taste when it is vulgar, offensive or blasphemous. Challenging convention is one thing; giving deliberate — perhaps even malicious — offence is another.

Introduction: what sort of material is in questionable taste?

As soon as one refers to 'the authorities', one thinks of the government. To be sure the government legislates against abuses in

Who are the 'authorities'?

response to shifts in public opinion — for example in respect of the use of long-lens photography to intrude into private lives; or it may liberalise the law, as in the context of consenting homosexuality. But censorship has most commonly been carried out by agencies more or less independent of the government, in the context of the law as it stands: the police, for example, who may raid the homes of those suspected of dealing in hard-core pornography; local councils who may forbid the showing of a particular film in local cinemas, as the Metropolitan Borough of Westminster did in banning the film *Crash*; and the British Board of Film Classification, which is charged with deciding which films are suitable for which audiences, and with labelling them accordingly.

The hope is that the producers of material for the stage, screen or press will practise self-censorship: that is, they will not seek to offend the public. Until 1968, new plays had to be submitted to the Lord Chamberlain for his approval before they could be staged. Theatre managers are free to stage what they like now — but because they want to attract 'family' audiences they choose not to risk losing their goodwill. The same goes for cinema chains: they have no interest in extremism. Film producers and directors know what they can get away with. The public knows what it can expect when a film is XX-rated. Should directors wish to gratify private tastes, they will produce films for showing in private clubs, whose patrons will not be offended. Still, self-censorship, as practised by Stanley Kubrick when he withdrew his own film *A Clockwork Orange* from the public arena, is highly unusual. He was the best qualified of all 'authorities' to take such action.

◀ Stage plays

◀ Films

◀ Self-censorship

Not all film directors exercise such restraint — and in this event, constraint may be justified. James Firman, when he retired as Chairman of the British Board of Film Classification, spoke of the sharp decline in the number of films, or the parts of films, that were candidates for censorship. We are more tolerant of nudity and 'sex scenes' than we were. But there is much that circulates in video format that never comes before the BBFC yet that, to all intents and purposes, is on general release. Most people would expect the authorities to control the availability (if they cannot prevent the production) of films involving sex with children and with animals, of the sort to which Firman referred. Unless we believe that 'anything goes', we must believe in some limits being placed on free expression.

◀ Restraint, or constraint

What should or should not appear in newspapers is a more difficult problem. There is no system of press censorship in Britain

— and it is something we can well do without, to judge by its baneful effects elsewhere. But the papers can be read by people of all ages and beliefs — they are not pre-classified, as films are. Editors have to exercise judgement on a daily basis. Columnists who make smutty or racist jokes will be quickly dropped — if the offensive jokes have not been edited out first. Page 3 girls in *The Sun* are not a serious issue either, since readers know they will be there, and can read an alternative newspaper if they choose. More contentious are photographs of the victims of accidents or war. The editor of *The Observer* courted controversy when he decided to run, over two pages, the famous picture taken by Kenneth Jarecke of an incinerated Iraqi soldier in the Gulf War. Editors had to exercise their judgement, too, in respect of Clinton's 'sexual relationship' (real or imagined) with White House aide Monica Lewinsky. What was it within the bounds of 'good taste' to divulge?

◁ The press: editorial judgement

The Calcutt Committee was set up in 1990 to consider complaints against such editorial judgements. And this is surely all the ex *post facto* censorship we need. Producers ought to be free to exercise their own judgement, according to publicly established guidelines; but there need to be 'watchdogs' to which the public can turn when producers overstep the threshold of what is acceptable.

◁ Conclusion

e To have asked candidates to comment knowledgeably in both (or all three) areas was a tall order. I have left the title and the essay as they are, both as an object lesson and as offering sufficient resources — in terms of ideas — for two or three potential essays.

I would make the same case again. I don't honestly think one could make a convincing case either for heavy-handed censorship on the one hand or for an ethical free-for-all on the other. Light-touch monitoring will always be called for.

AO4 The whole essay is about the limits of *certainty* in the context of public taste. Every culture has its threshold of tolerance, and so does every individual – so any answer to this question is bound to be *partial*.

Section 3 Arts

Popular music

Question

'Most popular music is written to a simple formula: it's synthesised by machine to produce mechanical emotional responses. It's a talent-free zone.' How would you answer this criticism of popular music?

There are several words in this 'criticism' that call for clarification:
(a) What is meant by 'popular' music?
(b) How simple is 'simple'?
(c) 'Machine' and 'mechanical' are loaded words calling for comment.
(d) How do we define 'talent'?

Consideration of these points might well occupy an extended introduction. Popular music (however it's defined) can probably absorb some of the criticism — a lot of popular music is pretty ordinary; but it can rebut some of the criticism too. Our two positions, therefore, are:

Position A
Yes, much popular music is simple — even lacking in talent.

Position B
Much music of all sorts is simple. Popular music should not be judged by its worst examples.

It might be expected that you will defend popular music against what is rather extreme criticism, and that your conclusion will be that though there is much dross, the best of popular music will survive.

Answer

The criticism makes a lot of assumptions about what certain words mean. By popular music, does the critic mean 'pop' music of the sort that features in the 'top ten', as measured by record sales? Much folk music, gypsy violin music, Scottish bagpipe music is written to a simple formula; but surely we do not criticise it on this ground. The simple formula is what makes much popular music what it is — but it is also what makes church hymn music, plain chant and madrigals what they are. A lot of modern concert-hall music makes a virtue of simplicity too: the work of Steve Reich, Philip Glass and Arvo Part among minimalists comes to mind.

Synthesised music is 'mechanical', to be sure; but it is not mechanical in the same sense that a musical box or a barrel organ are mechanical. There is no more talent needed to operate these than

◁ Introduction: questions about definition. What is 'popular' and what is 'simple'?

◁ What is 'mechanical' music?

there is to put a record on a turntable. A synthesiser does have to be operated by someone with a musical ear, just as Apple Macintosh design software has to be exploited by someone with an artistic eye.

It is a virtue of much popular music that it is simple. It is not talent-free by virtue of its simplicity alone. 'Talent' is a difficult word to define, but one might be said to be talented when one is good at what one does. Thus the best popular-songwriters are talented; even, it may be said, the best performers — on electric guitar, drums or at the synthesiser keyboard — are talented.

◀ What do we mean by 'talent'?

Of course, there is much popular music that falls a long way short of 'the best'. How could it be otherwise? More music is written, recorded and performed, and more recorded music is bought to be listened to by more people, than ever before. It is a very big, very profitable industry, so it is inevitable that a lot of what is produced is of indifferent quality. Certain bands enjoy such success — and such sudden wealth — that large numbers of young people form themselves into bands in the hope that they will strike it rich also. Some of it will be 'popular' for a while, but little of it will last. The irony is that what does last, what proves to be most popular, is likely to be music (of its kind) of the highest quality.

◀ Position A: much popular music is lacking in talent

Quantity is perhaps the enemy of quality, in one sense. More generally does mean worse. On the other hand, the more music — good, bad and indifferent — that there is, the more likely it is that some of it will prove to have lasting qualities. We do not listen to every one of Haydn's 106 symphonies with equal attention, but if he had not written as many as this we should not have had No. 88 or No. 102, for instance. Would anyone with an interest in music want to discourage anyone else from making music if there was any chance that they might produce something half-way worthwhile? William Wordsworth produced a lot of poetry in a long life: much of it is no longer read, but we do not judge him by this token to be lacking in talent. Likewise, we do not judge Frank Sinatra as a singer, Louis Armstrong as a jazz trumpeter, or Cole Porter as a songwriter by their worst work; we judge them by their best, and we acknowledge them to have been enormously talented.

◀ Position B: popular music cannot be so lightly dismissed

Music that is 'synthesised by machine' is unlikely to be very distinguished as music. Perhaps, therefore, it ought not to be criticised as music. It has a practical function, and a highly particular context. In a recent opinion poll, the music of the Beatles was judged to have had the most impact in our time. We can only safely make this judgement after nearly 40 years of listening to it. The most acute critic of all time is time itself.

◀ Conclusion: let time be the judge

Essays

e The danger, in an essay such as this, in response to a title such as this, is that a middle-class, middle-aged, white Anglo-Saxon male writer will be (or seem to be) 'out of touch'. I would ask who it is who could be said to be in touch — who is best qualified to offer a view on this subject? Whose view could be said to be authoritative? — but I would accept the criticism, all the same. The views that I have expressed in the essay are irredeemably those of a 'has-been' (or 'never was').

AO4 And, as such, they are *partial*. Anyone's views – in response to the *subjective opinion* quoted in the question – is bound to be partial. In being explicit about this, you will raise your mark.

Section 3: Social Sciences

Religion and moral values

Question

It is sometimes said that we live in a 'moral vacuum' — that we are confused about moral values. How far is this connected, in your view, with the decline in religious belief?

There are two questions here:
(a) Do we live in a moral vacuum?
(b) If so, is this because of the decline in religious belief? (The question appears to assume this decline. Certainly churchgoing has declined — but you may want to say in your conclusion that this is a poor index of religious belief.)

You could take up one of two positions:

Position A
That we do live in a moral vacuum.

Position B
That we don't live in a moral vacuum.

I shall take up position B, but will refer to position A in my introduction. I shall go on to give reasons for asserting that we do not live in a moral vacuum. I shall then have to address the second question, about religious belief.

Answer

When people say: 'we live in a moral vacuum', they usually mean that young people, in particular, are not being given the moral guidance in the home or at school that a former generation was given. They point to the number of divorces and otherwise broken homes as evidence of a general moral breakdown of which young people are the principal victims. People who take this view often point to the passing not only of religious belief, but of deference to authority of the sort that used to remind parishioners of the Ten Commandments, and hold out either the promise of heaven or the threat of hell.

    It might be argued that we do not live in a moral vacuum, however. One only has to read the local press covering any town or county in the land, to read of tragic incidents; and a trawl of local newspapers in county record offices will yield a multitude of horror stories, every bit as gruesome as those we read about today. Social historians bear witness to the prevalence of armed gangs, highway robberies, infanticides, garrottings, and 'disappearances' in the days

Introduction: Position A

Position B: reason (a) — there has always been 'immoral behaviour'

AS/A-Level General Studies

before there was a police force to prevent them and a press to report on them. There is nothing new under the sun.

We know more of the grisly details about sordid events — such as the activities of Frederick and Rosemary West of Gloucester — precisely because the newspapers make so much of them, and because television and radio news broadcasts fill whatever gaps in our knowledge the newspapers might have left. The result is that we imagine that the moral health of the nation is far worse than it is — and than it was.

> Reason (b) — news coverage

We should not, in any case, draw the conclusion from a few high-profile cases of wicked behaviour that society as a whole is going to the dogs. What evidence is there for suggesting that we are all confused about moral values; or — if we are — that we are more confused now than we were, say, a generation or two ago? Did our parents and their parents live in moral fresh air when they shot the shell-shocked for desertion in the First World War? When they hanged convicted murderers? When they outlawed suicides and vilified homosexuals? It could almost be said of the present that we are more tolerant now, more humane — more moral — than our parents and grandparents were. But such comparisons are invidious, and not easily sustained.

> Reason (c) — it is misleading to argue that the actions of a few can be attributed to the majority (Questions of this sort force the opposition onto the defensive.)

It is true, of course, that more marriages do end in divorce these days; that children are often shunted between father and mother or are brought up in single-parent households, ignorant of who their genetic father (or more rarely mother) might be. This is a relatively new social development with which we are having to learn to cope. On the other hand, is it evident that a child who is brought up by a single mother — abandoned, perhaps, by her partner — will grow up less moral than in a family where the father was violent, sexually abusive, dissolute or merely neglectful? The families who stayed together before the passing of the 1968 Divorce Reform Act were not necessarily better moral nurseries than families of today who can exercise choice.

> Reason (d) — social circumstances are different, but not necessarily worse

If we are more confused about moral values it is likely to be because we do have more choice — and one cannot be truly moral unless one is free to choose one's course of action. It is a combination of technology and law reform that have given us this choice — the technologies of reliable contraception, safe abortion techniques, embryo research, genetic engineering, 'smart' weaponry and the like.

> A concession on 'moral confusion' — but a positive view

Religion probably doesn't come into it. We may be less religious than we were (though the number of people going to church is a

> Conclusion

Section 3

> poor indicator of religious belief, just as the number of hospital admissions is an imperfect measure of public health) — or less outwardly so. But how many people have ever been made more moral than they would otherwise be by being preached at or prayed over? Religious belief does not make one moral; it sanctions moral behaviour. Whether or not one is moral has more to do with what goes on in the home, and other social contexts, than with what happens in the pew.

◁ This is a personal view, of course — but this is what is asked for. Yours might be quite different, and not be wrong.

e The title may suggest the need for a balance between the 'moral vacuum' question and the 'decline in religious belief' question. My answer certainly doesn't keep this balance. I don't think I needed to say anything more under Position A: the introduction was a perfectly proper place for expressing disagreement with that position.

I could have chosen two quite different positions:

Position A
The moral vacuum is associated with the decline of religion.

Position B
The moral vacuum has other origins than the decline of religion.

but I wanted to question the very notion of our living in a moral vacuum. It was not a claim that I could accept, and then account for. I wanted to argue against the claim; therefore, the 'decline of religion' point was bound to be reduced in importance.

AO4 As I say in the margin, at the end, this is a personal view. Any moral/religious question will invite a personal response. To be respectable, however, any *opinion* must be based on publicly available evidence. Anyone arguing that religion fostered moral certainty would have to explain the Victorian treatment of non-whites and of women.

Section 3 Social Sciences

Comprehensive schooling

Question

The comprehensive school was introduced in order that all children, of all races and religions, rich and poor, clever and not-so-clever, should be educated together. Do you think this is still a worthwhile ideal?

> It would probably be as well, in a brief introduction, to explain the system that the comprehensive school replaced. We have here a (fairly) simple clash of ideologies: the comprehensive school was a feature of Labour Party thinking, whose object was to equalise opportunity. It opposed Conservative Party support for selection. More recently, we have what some would say is a messy compromise.
>
> These two ideologies effectively divide the essay into two halves:
>
> **Position A**
> The case for selection, and for different types of school.
>
> **Position B**
> The case for the comprehensive school and equality of opportunity.
>
> I shall examine the two positions in this order, both because this makes historical sense and because the introduction will lead straight into Position A and the conclusion will follow straight from Position B.

Answer

The Butler Act of 1944 introduced the '11+' examination so that all children had a chance to go to the grammar school. Pupils who failed went on to the new secondary modern schools. Irrespective of success or failure at the 11+, there was to be 'secondary education for all'.

◁ Introduction: the situation before 1965

This was felt to be a fair and meritocratic system. All but a few children of richer parents who attended private preparatory schools went to the same primary schools — so everyone received the same teaching. In theory, therefore, all had an equal chance of passing the 11+; and, in fact, many children from working-class families did pass the exam and take up places in grammar schools. The 'clever' children were thus taught, in the grammar schools, by graduate teachers; and they were able to study classical and modern languages, and laboratory sciences that were not on offer in most secondary modern schools. What is more, they were able to study with each other: weak pupils did not hold clever ones

◁ Position A: the case for selection in a meritocracy. An argument that stresses the benefit to the pupils

Question and Answer Guide

back, therefore they learned at a faster pace than would have been possible in an all-ability school.

Conservative thinkers might also have had social and economic motives for supporting the 11+. The theory was that the economy needed a professional class of managers, lawyers, doctors, academics and financiers. These could be supplied by the grammar schools. A layer of technicians, engineers, foremen and craftspeople was also needed — and these would be the products of the (rather fewer than intended) technical schools. The secondary modern schools would supply the economy with an army of no less necessary employees: nurses, factory operatives, shop workers and clerical personnel.

> An argument that stresses the benefits to society and the economy

The fact that society and the economy have changed is not the least important reason why the 11+ had to go. A Labour government circular of 1965 instructed councils to consider ways in which their schools might 'go comprehensive'. It had long been recognised that the 11+ exam did not merely sort children into the 'clever' and the not-so-clever; it divided them according to social class. Many working-class children who passed did not thrive in the grammar schools; and many 'late-developing' middle- (and working-) class children found themselves marooned in secondary modern schools. Eleven was too early to make a decision that would affect children's education and employment chances for the rest of their lives. The 11+ did not grant equality of opportunity: it gave an advantage to those children who were ready for it, and for whom there were grammar school places available — and such places were by no means evenly spread.

> Position B: the 11+ exam was, in many ways, an inefficient device. The individual argument reversed

True equality of opportunity demands that doors be kept open much longer. What is more, society and the economy demand it. The labour market has ceased to be stratified in the old way: technology is changing so fast that we need a flexible workforce, capable of developing multiple skills — and of re-skilling when necessary. This is the situation in the present, and it will be the situation in the future.

> The social–economic argument reversed

Britain is plural; multicultural; diverse. We cannot know any longer (if we ever could) what we would be selecting pupils for. They all need the same education service just as they all need the same health service. There are those who still call for 'freedom of choice' of different schools, competing with each other for the 'best' pupils. This would inevitably mean selection. Surely a real freedom of choice will enable pupils to elect their courses rather than to be selected for them and — all too likely — to be rejected.

> Conclusion: a plea for real freedom of choice

Essays

> I think I represent the pro-selection ideology (Position A) reasonably fairly — indeed, I perhaps under-represent two of the most significant reasons why middle-class parents choose to send their children to selective schools: (a) the fear that 'clever' children would be outnumbered by not-so-clever children, and be held back, if they were all in the same school (even in the same class); and (b) the fear that 'nice' middle-class children would be educated alongside less well-brought-up children who would be a bad influence.

AO4 It is difficult to be *impartial* where this topic is concerned. Even many of those who support the comprehensive school in principle, seek out a selective school for their own children, in practice. It is an issue in which our social *values* are tested to the utmost.

Section 3 Social Sciences

Trial by jury

Question

Trial by jury is customary in British courts of law. What seem to you to be the advantages and disadvantages of this system?

> The essay falls naturally into three parts:
> (a) The origins of, reasons behind and nature of the jury system
> (b) Its advantages
> (c) Its disadvantages
>
> Quite a lot of information will need to be given before the argument can be weighed. This is not a law essay, however, so there is no question of your needing to know anything about specific cases; but some knowledge of the sort that is in the public domain will be expected. You will 'answer' the question in parts (b) and (c) — but you will need to form a judgement one way or the other in your conclusion, or declare the pros and cons to be evenly balanced.

Answer

The jury has its origin in the need for local people to come forward with background knowledge of a case, and of the defendant in that case. The judge would travel about the country, so he would have little knowledge of the historical, geographical and other circumstances of a particular area. He would probably know little about local customs — and it is on custom that the apparatus of English law has been built. Twelve men (and they were always men) were chosen who could supply knowledge of this local sort.

The judge directed the jurors in regard to matters of law and the conduct of the case. It was their job to put forward matters of fact that bore upon the case, and — more importantly — to decide whether or not the defendant was guilty. The judge would then pass the appropriate sentence. Trial by jury replaced trial by ordeal (if defendants could endure the physical tests by which they were challenged, they were acquitted) and other mechanisms for deciding guilt or innocence that were not based on reasoned enquiry. The tradition was that defendants would choose to be tried by their peers, by 'twelve good men and true', who knew them or understood what might have driven them to commit an offence.

Introduction: origins of the jury and reasons behind it

Essays

> The nature of the jury system

Nowadays more than 95% of cases, civil and criminal, are heard in magistrates' courts. It is only the more serious criminal cases that are heard in the crown courts, by circuit judges, where a defendant can elect to be tried by jury — and then a jury is only called if the defendant pleads not guilty. Historically, a jury had to be unanimous in its verdict — but because it was felt that a failure to reach a verdict led to too many acquittals of 'guilty' persons, the law was changed in 1968. Since that time, majority verdicts (of 10:2) have been accepted. Any registered voter between the ages of 18 and 70 may serve on a jury, provided he, or now she, has been living in the UK for at least 5 years, is not a member of the clergy, a convicted criminal, a law officer or one who has been certified insane.

> 1st advantage of the jury system

It remains a powerful argument for the jury system that ordinary people are judged by ordinary people, and not by aristocrats or a class of professional lawyers operating at a social–intellectual distance from those whom they are trying. It is to this extent a 'democratic' system.

> 2nd advantage

> 3rd advantage

It is a sound principle of justice that there should be a distinction made between the facts in a case and matters of law — perhaps matters of a quite technical sort. Thus, if a jury — having weighed the facts of a case and having appraised the defendant's motives and character — find him or her not guilty, no amount of legal argument can override the jury's verdict. The judge is bound to acquit. This is a context in which there is safety in numbers, since 12 people are more likely to come to an accurate judgement of guilt or innocence than one (sometimes, it has to be said) idiosyncratic individual.

> 4th advantage

Finally, jurors do an important citizen's duty when doing jury service, and in return for this participation they learn valuable lessons about the system to which we are all subject.

> 1st disadvantage

Perhaps the most significant disadvantage of the jury system is the expense involved in recruiting, and perhaps accommodating, 12 individuals with lives of their own to lead. It undoubtedly adds to the time that a trial may take and therefore — again — to the cost. Justice deferred, they say, is justice denied.

> 2nd disadvantage

> 3rd disadvantage

The jury room is a 'black box': no one knows what goes on inside it. Have the members of the jury understood what they have seen and heard? Sometimes a case can throw up very complex issues — not merely legal, but psychological, neurological, forensic, to say nothing of ethical, issues. By definition, lay jurors are expert in none of these matters. Have they truly agreed on the verdict, or have one or two individuals browbeaten them into agreement?

> 4th disadvantage

> Have they, indeed, been overawed by directions that the judge has given them? After all, a judge decides what the jury may or may not hear under the rules of evidence; and the judge can give a steer to the verdict that he wants the jury to return in his summing up. A jury will not lightly discount the authoritative view of an expert and experienced judge. ◀ 5th disadvantage
>
> But perhaps they should not. The judge and jury share power according to well-established formulae. Maybe a jury should be called only in very serious cases; but the principle is a sound one. If it was not, it would not have lasted as long as it has. ◀ Conclusion

e Four advantages and five disadvantages of the jury system are rather more of both than you might be expected to think of.

I should mention here that I have omitted reference in the essay to civil cases of defamation. Though these are often jury trials, they throw up issues of another sort than could reasonably have been included in an essay of examination length.

AO4 The point is made that the jury is charged with coming to a verdict on the basis of the *facts* of the case. Originally, the jury would have supplied local *knowledge*; now, they supply a sort of common-sense, person-in-the-street knowledge that a judge may lack. The verdict may, ultimately, be an *opinion*, but at least it is a consensus of ten or twelve opinions, and not just (the judge's) one.

Section 3 Social Sciences

Our duty to vote

Question

Only a minority of those who are eligible now bother to vote in local and European elections. Why do you think this is, and how far do you agree that it is our duty to vote in elections at local, national and international levels?

> We shall need some simple facts about voting patterns by way of introduction. What proportion of the electorate does vote in local and government elections? Next, we shall need to address the question why so few people 'bother to vote'. Then it is time to consider the issue of 'duty':
>
> **Position A**
> It is our duty to vote in elections.
>
> **Position B**
> It is not our duty to vote. It is our choice.
>
> You will need to come to a conclusion one way or the other — or both. The words 'how far ...' in the question are an invitation to non-commitment. It is enough to weigh up the two sets of arguments and find merit on both sides.

Answer

We vote for councillors at district or county level; for MPs to the House of Commons at national level; and for Members of the European Parliament. Scotland has its own election to the Scottish Parliament, in Edinburgh; and Wales its election to the Welsh Assembly, in Cardiff. ◁ *Introduction: the range of elections*

In 1997, in the election which returned the Labour Party to power with a majority in the Commons of 178 seats, the turn-out was 71%; in 2001, it was reduced to 59%. Only 60% of Scottish voters cast their votes in the referendum for a Scottish Parliament; in Wales, only just over half (51%) bothered to vote. ◁ *What proportion of the electorate does vote?*

Local elections, of one sort or another, come round more frequently. For these, and for European elections, voter turn-out drops to something like one third, or less, of the electorate. One can put low turn-outs for European elections down to Euroscepticism, or to the perception that MEPs are remote (constituencies are large, so the relationship between a member and his or her constituents can seldom be close), and that they live in style at our expense. But surely these reasons for voter apathy do not apply at the district level? It is a common perception that local government has few powers following 18 years of centralising tendencies under ◁ *Why do so few people bother to vote?*

the Conservatives — and as few voters know their councillors as know their MEPs. Only during the party razzmatazz of Westminster elections, it seems, do voters see the candidates with their own eyes. The media, too, whip up public interest in general elections, of a sort that is lacking at local and international levels. There is no escaping the advertising and the controversy when seats in the Commons are at stake.

Many people fought for our right to vote; perhaps we owe it to them to exercise the right for which they campaigned. We live in a liberal democracy; maybe we owe it to those who live under repressive regimes not to take our freedom to vote for granted. If we do not exercise our rights, we might one day find that we have lost them. If we do not vote, we are in no position to object to what our elected representatives do in our name. We give them enormous power over our lives, so we owe it to ourselves and to each other to monitor and to moderate the exercise of that power. We have only ourselves to blame if it is abused.

> Position A: it is our duty to vote

On the other hand, would we want to be compelled to vote, as in Australia? Surely if the emphasis is placed on its being our civic duty, rather than our right, to vote, there is a risk that we may resent having to do so. In a free society we should be as free to withhold our vote as to cast it. Indeed, in refusing to vote we issue a very potent challenge to politicians to do more to rouse our interest and encourage our commitment. Something has gone wrong when only one third of electors 'bother to vote'. The fault may not all lie on the side of the voters — indeed, it is said that voters would take more interest in elections if there were a more proportionate relationship between the number of votes cast for a party and the number of seats that party wins. Under the present first-past-the-post system a large proportion of the votes is perceived to be 'wasted'. People will not turn out at elections if they believe that their vote will make little or no difference.

> Position B: it is not our duty; it is our choice

A healthy democracy is one in which all 'stakeholders' are involved. Current low turn-out figures suggest that the system is in need of reform. Life can be more satisfying when one is in control of it; to surrender control of it to others leads to cynicism and even alienation. A liberal democracy cannot afford to let that sort of rot set in.

> Conclusion

e It is worth adding that the title might have had a different emphasis: it might have focused on the concern that has been expressed in some quarters that young people, in particular, are not registering to vote in the first place — and so debarring themselves from engaging in the political process from the start.

AO4 This is another subject on which it is difficult to be *impartial*. The voting figures are *facts* (that you would not be expected to know); but I have expressed *opinions* about 'liberal democracy', about compulsory voting, and about proportional representation. I have to acknowledge that it is perfectly possible to adhere to democratic *values,* and yet hold different views as to how democracy might be achieved.

Section 3 Sciences

Electrically powered rail transport

Question

'An electrically powered rail transport system offers big environmental advantages over other forms of transport.' What evidence is there to support or refute this statement?

No AS/A-level student — not even a physicist or a geographer — is likely to have specialist knowledge to bring to this question. Besides, a General Studies essay is intended to be accessible to the intelligent layperson. You certainly don't need to know anything about the workings of an electrically powered rail transport system in order to answer this question.

We have here a title in which we can identify two positions, but one that also suggests a list approach:

Position A
Support for the statement
1st piece of evidence
2nd piece of evidence
etc.

Position B
Refutation of the statement
1st piece of evidence
2nd piece of evidence
etc.

The question does not itself tend either way. It is genuinely open to you to come to a conclusion one way or the other.

I shall, broadly, support the statement because I can think of rather few reasons for opposing it.

Answer

An electrically powered rail transport system would once have meant either heavy-duty trains running on wide track-beds between major towns and cities, or trams such as those that survive on Blackpool promenade. Nowadays, such a system is likely to suggest the sort of urban light railway that serves the City of Manchester and London Docklands.

> Introduction: a brief definition of what we are talking about

Such a system is able to carry large numbers of passengers at a time, so that — particularly at peak hours — a good deal of road-space is saved that would otherwise be given over to large

> Support for the statement: 1st piece of 'evidence'

Essays

numbers of buses and cars. These cause congestion, which in turn lengthens journey times. Furthermore, buses and cars are a danger to cyclists and pedestrians, whereas rail transport can be kept physically separate from other road users, on easily identifiable tracks. These tracks can be laid above, below or quite apart from the level of conventional roads.

When we speak of the 'environment', however, we usually think of the appearance of the landscape, the quality of the air we breathe and the sustainability of the technology that we put in place. Of course, the very fact that there would be fewer motor vehicles on urban roads would make streetscapes pleasanter to look at, and reduce the need for so much space to be devoted to parking as at present. There would be less need for the building of new roads, for the widening and upgrading of existing roads and for the road markings, signs, sliproads and fly-overs that have done so much to deface the urban and suburban landscape in recent years.

Diesel- and petrol-burning vehicles pose still more insidious dangers for our health, and for the long-term health of the planet. Petrol engines emit carbon monoxide (CO), nitrogen oxide (NO_x), carbon dioxide (CO_2) and particulate matter. Diesel engines are thought to be responsible for rising levels of particulates (or PM_{10}) in the air we breathe. Nitrogen oxide is a potent source of the problem of 'acid rain', which erodes the stonework of some of our finest buildings and causes trees to die back in forests many miles downwind of British cities. Nitrogen oxide reacts with sunlight to increase concentrates of ozone at ground level — and this cocktail may cause problems for asthma sufferers, particularly among children, for many of whom puffers and inhalers have joined the pens and books and indoor shoes in their school bags. Catalytic converters can remove the NO_x, the CO and the bigger particulates from vehicle emissions, but not the carbon dioxide; CO_2 is a big contributor to global warming, or climate change.

Oil, of course, is a fossil fuel which — quite apart from the pollution caused by burning it — is a dwindling asset. The electricity to power trams or light railways could be generated in coal- or gas-fired stations, or by nuclear power. On the other hand coal and gas are also fossil fuels, and nuclear power poses other problems. We are in danger of shifting the pollution from city streets to the power-stations — to whose number we should have to add, perhaps quite significantly. Indeed, whatever means of generating electricity was chosen (sustainable or not), we should

◀ 2nd piece of evidence — and sharpening of environmental focus

◀ 3rd piece of evidence — perhaps the crucial element of the supporting case

(You probably do need to know the basic facts about vehicle emissions. Global warming is a standard topic on General Studies papers nowadays.)

◀ 4th piece of supporting evidence

◀ 1st piece of evidence to refute the statement

> have to accept a growth in number of electricity sub-stations, pylons and similar infrastructure.
>
> Until we are able to harness the power of sunlight more efficiently we must accept that all forms of mass transit carry negative environmental implications. Still, on balance, an electrically powered rail transport system has significant advantages for the environment over other forms of transport.

◁ 2nd piece of evidence in refutation

◁ A conclusion that makes use of the words in the essay title

e This is a relatively brief essay, perhaps because I felt there was less of an 'argument' to conduct than elsewhere. On a second reading, I would have to concede to the criticism that I didn't make enough of the comparison called for in the title ('... over other forms of transport'). I compared light rail systems with urban road transport — its most obvious competitor — but not with water-borne transport, nor with aircraft.

AO4 Science is not *value*-free. It is not all inert *facts*. The science (a word we use for *knowledge* acquired methodically) in General Studies is certainly open to *opinion*. Road-builders, motorists, environmentalists all see this issue from a point of view – but it is fair to say that environmentalists do try to adopt the point of view of the planet.

Section 3 Sciences

Scientifically modified food

Question

There is some anxiety about the extent to which the food that we eat is being modified by science for commercial reasons. How far would you say such anxiety is justified?

Three kinds of modification come to mind:
   (a) The addition of colorants, preservatives and flavourings
   (b) Irradiation
   (c) Genetic engineering

This is probably a case where Positions A (food modification is safe) and B (there is cause for anxiety) are best interleaved with the three kinds of modification. Thus, the essay will look like this:
   (a) Additives (A: case for) ⟶ (B: doubts about)
   (b) Irradiation (A) ⟶ (B)
   (c) Genetic engineering (A) ⟶ (B)

At the end of which we can only hope to return a rather open verdict.

Answer

Food has been modified in a number of ways for a very long time — but such modification has increased as food has been mass-produced and sold in large retail outlets to a growing population. In this essay we will look in turn at food additives, irradiation and genetic engineering.

◀ Introduction: a statement of intent

In the processes of cooking and keeping, food loses some of its natural colour and flavour. 'Natural' colour can be reintroduced: caramel (or burnt sugar) can be added to give food a dark brown colour; chlorophyll extract can be added to lime marmalade, for example, to enhance its natural-looking greenness. We are familiar with carotene to make food yellow and cochineal or beetroot to make it red. Few will object to these additives — indeed, we should be much more likely to object to their absence, since untreated food would look quite unappetising. Artificial sweeteners and monosodium glutamate are major flavour enhancers. These are substitutes for sugar and salt respectively. Too much of either of the real thing is unhealthy, so the substitutes are held by the food

◀ (a) Food additives: Position A

industry to be safer. Finally, preservatives like sorbic acid and sulphur dioxide are added to food to improve its keeping properties. When food is grown in one place, processed in another, sold in a third and stored in the larder or fridge before it is consumed, we have no option but to ensure that it has a safe, extended 'shelf life'.

◀ Position B

There need be no anxiety about most food additives. They are only approved after exhaustive tests, and their use is strictly regulated. Some, like the preservatives acetic acid and sorbic acid, have been around for so long that we can be confident about them. The yellow colorant Tartrazine, on the other hand, was implicated in hyperactivity in children. The cause–effect relationship was never proved, but public disquiet was sufficient to have it withdrawn. It is not so much particular additives that worry the experts, it is the sheer number of them ingested over a long period that is worrying. We simply have no means of knowing what their long-term effects may be, not only on our health, but on our behaviour also.

◀ (b) Irradiation:

Certain foods may be irradiated either to kill bacteria that may spoil them, or to rescue food that is already contaminated in some way. Gamma rays, or electron beams, damage the DNA of bacteria and viruses. Salmonella, for example, a notorious cause of food poisoning in chickens, is easily eliminated by irradiation, permitting them to be stored for longer in supermarket refrigerators. However, not all bacteria are killed by the irradiation process; and even when they are, the toxins that they give rise to may not be. Furthermore, irradiation may be effective at the time, but as the process is intended to extend the life of the food item (and prolong its journey from producer to consumer) we cannot tell what ill effects it may have on the nutritional value of the food by the time it is subjected to yet more radiation in the microwave.

◀ Position A

◀ Position B

◀ (c) Genetic engineering:

But the most potent source of anxiety centres on genetic engineering. This is where the genetic code (or DNA) of a single plant, or animal, cell is altered and made the basis of new growth — and transmitted to subsequent generations. Thus, when we have identified the genes responsible for harmful viruses — like the red stripe virus in strains of rice — they can be eliminated by radiation from the DNA, generating plants resistant to the virus. It goes without saying, though, that exposing cells to X-rays, or introducing chemicals, is a very sensitive and potentially very damaging procedure. We cannot be sure that only the target gene is affected, and that we shall not engineer a rogue mutation that will enter the

◀ Position A

◀ Position B

germ-line with disastrous consequences. We cannot be confident that we have god-like control of a technology that is so relatively new, when the genetic material we seek to alter is so very complex. There is something dangerously hit-and-miss about the process — and because the companies concerned invest so much research funding in prolonged experiments there is a good deal of secrecy involved, and patenting of life forms for commercial advantage.

If there is no room for moral panic, there is room for anxiety. Fools rush in where angels would fear to tread.

◁ Conclusion

> I confess to having had to do a spot of homework in order to be able to write this essay — just as I should have had to do if I had been teaching this topic. Food science is not a subject in which I feel wonderfully confident. My research did not extend beyond a simple book from my local library, and a few labels on food products, however.
>
> If I have made mistakes where matters of fact are concerned and you are able to identify them, you are better placed than I was to answer this question. There may be other ways in which our food is modified that I have not mentioned.
>
> **AO4** I have expressed rather few *opinions* here, mostly because I felt it necessary to be in possession of *facts*. There is room for *bias* if one is involved in the food industry, however; we should attach particular *value* to the work of scientists who are independent of the industry.

Section 3 Sciences

Renewable energy

Question

What are the practical advantages, and difficulties, of developing any two ways of generating electricity from renewable, non-nuclear sources?

The essay will fall naturally into four parts, and all will be of roughly the same length:

First renewable energy source	Second renewable energy source
Advantages	Advantages
Difficulties	Difficulties

You might list the most significant renewable sources of energy in your introduction, then choose the two about which you have most to say. There is no overall question to answer, so there is little call for anything in the nature of a conclusion.

Answer

Renewable energy sources are those that are in infinite supply. Fossil fuels, such as coal, oil and gas, are obtained by mining or drilling, from rock strata deep under the land surface. Reserves of these fuels are steadily diminishing. The principal renewable fuel sources are geothermal heat, sea tides and waves, the wind, the sun (solar power), and hydroelectric power. In this essay I shall discuss wind and hydroelectric power.

◀ Introduction: a definition and a list

The first obvious advantage of harnessing wind power is that there is a lot of it. In fact, for its size Britain is the windiest country in Europe. After many years and many millions of pounds' worth of research, an efficient turbine is now in production. Computer technology ensures that the 30-metre-long blades face into the prevailing wind, whilst a brake is automatically applied to shut down the mechanism in a wind strong enough to do damage. Wind turbines can be sited on windy uplands — of which the UK has an abundance; or they can be built on platforms on the sea-bed in deep shallows along the shoreline, where the wind blows strongest. Clusters of wind turbines — in so-called 'wind farms' —

◀ Wind power — advantages:

◀ efficiency

already feed significant resources of electricity into the national grid. They do not require the building of costly and unsightly power-stations in anyone's 'back yard' — indeed there are those who find the slim white turbines quite beautiful, and their slowly turning blades almost moving. But not the least significant advantage of wind turbines is that they are entirely non-polluting. They release no harmful emissions into the air, soil or water courses.

It has to be said that not everyone finds wind turbines, either singly or in clusters, particularly attractive. Offshore they spoil the view of the open sea, and on land, they disfigure some of our finest wild hill country. They are often sited on the edges of national parks, on hill crests where they can be seen for miles around. Such technology, however 'advanced', is simply out of place in what is left of our countryside. At the same time, they cannot be sited close to where people live because they make a constant, irritating whirring noise. Ecologists have warned of the possibly harmful effects on seal-breeding and nesting sites of installing turbines on huge concrete piles along the coast; and on land, turbines have to be sited well away from trees because they interfere with wind flow. It has been estimated that by the year 2025 some 10% of our energy might be supplied by wind turbines; but this presupposes public acceptance of hundreds and hundreds of new wind farms — and we still have to meet 90% of our needs in other, perhaps more conventional, ways.

There is nothing new about water power, of course: a flow of water over a millwheel has long powered some quite heavy machinery; but turbines to generate electricity in commercial quantities require a massive head of water. This can be provided by damming a river, and so creating a vast lake with a head of between 900 and 1,500 metres. The upland areas of Wales, Scotland and northern England, where there are deep valleys and predictable rainfall, offered many suitable sites for hydroelectric power-stations. These may not have necessitated the building of a dam, since a high head of water could be piped to lower levels to yield as much power as damming a low head of water (of perhaps 9–30 metres). Apart from the electrical power produced, hydroelectric projects can be undertaken in concert with flood-control, irrigation and water-supply measures. Hydroelectric power-stations are clean, and emit no harmful gases into the atmosphere.

A major problem with hydroelectric power is that there is a limit to the number of potential sites for power-stations — and

Margin notes: objects of beauty; non-polluting; Disadvantages:; unsightly; noise; insufficiency; Hydroelectricity — advantages:; availability; water services; non-polluting; Disadvantages:

> that limit has been more or less reached in the UK. There is understandable resistance to the flooding of populated, agriculturally rich or wooded valleys. Furthermore, water flow in the UK rivers fluctuates with the seasons. A station with a capacity equal to dry-weather water flow returns a small power output, and most of the flow is wasted. In exceptionally dry conditions (and we have experienced these in recent years) a power-station runs at well below its capacity, and is therefore grossly inefficient. Wildlife habitats and fish stocks are likely to be affected by dam and reservoir building, though some species may be beneficiaries. It is vital that tree cover be maintained on the slopes above the water line, otherwise soils are eroded and accumulate, causing siltation of the reservoir and a reduction in power-station efficiency. Whilst hydroelectric power is likely to continue to be important in certain areas — in central Africa, and at Niagara Falls, for example — suitable sites are very unevenly distributed, therefore large-scale projects are unlikely to be the pattern for the future.

◁ fluctuating supply

◁ ecology

◁ siltation

e The problem of energy supply, and the exploitation of renewable and fossil sources of energy, is a staple of General Studies 'science' questions — so some basic knowledge about and understanding of the issue is vital. Its saliency in General Studies specifications may even be thought of as a powerful argument for General Studies, since it might otherwise go missing from the 16–19 curriculum.

With six renewable sources to choose from (and I might conceivably have missed one) my pairing of wind and hydroelectric energy sources is one of 15 possible pairings — but none of the other 14 possibilities is likely to look very different from the essay that I have written. In all cases, the advantages are an infinity of supply (with the reservations that I have entered where hydroelectricity is concerned) and freedom from pollution; and the disadvantages are likely to be siting, negative effects on ecology, design and cost implications, predictability of supply, and amount of energy yield.

AO4 Again, there are *values* embedded in this topic – but it is not one where there is much fundamental disagreement, aside from the issue about whether wind turbines are considered elegant or not. But different parties to the debate will have different *biases*.

Section 3 Sciences

Computer technology

Question

Computer technology has revolutionised the ways in which we do business. Evaluate whether the developments taking place are all to the good.

> As usual, we need to present some facts before we can offer any opinions. We have to identify some ways in which computer technology has 'revolutionised' business. A list of three or four such ways will be enough.
>
> Only when we have presented these facts (if you can back them up with some figures, so much the better — but this is unlikely) can we proceed to evaluation, and to the two positions:
>
> **Position A**
> The developments have been 'good' — or good for the most part.
>
> **Position B**
> The developments have been 'bad' in certain important respects.
>
> It is likely that you will conclude that computer technology has increased the efficiency of 'the ways in which we do business', but that there have been some unfortunate social consequences. This would seem to be the common finding.

Answer

What computer technology is it that has 'revolutionised the way in which we do business'? It principally concerns the means by which information is stored, retrieved, handled, presented and communicated. With every new development in information technology the amount of data that the system can deal with grows, and the speed of all operations increases.

Information (in digital form) can be stored in the computer's central processing unit (CPU), or 'memory', in read-only (ROM) or random-access (RAM) form. Further backing stores can be added by means of hard discs, floppy discs and CD-ROMs. Hard discs can store large numbers of files, and access to them is very fast. Compact discs cannot (normally) be written to in the same way, but they can store considerably more data than floppy discs and are exchangeable and easy to transport. CDs, of course, can also store video and audio data.

The searching, sorting and analysis of data are all operations that can very swiftly be carried out at the keyboard, and on screen. A

◁ Introduction: define the term 'computer technology' in the business context

◁ The facilities offered by computer technology (or ICT)

◁ Position A: developments that have been 'good' for business

company might buy in a ready-made database on CD-ROM; it might create its own organisational database, in which is stored all the customer, supplier, costs and quality information that is of importance to the company; or it might subscribe to one or more remote on-line databases by modem. Public viewdata networks, such as the Internet, are interactive and open up the possibilities of electronic mail (e-mail) and electronic conferencing.

Word-processing and desk-top publishing facilities enable information to be presented by an 'electronic office' in ways that could only have been dreamt of a few years ago. Print quality, layout and typography are routinely of a sort that would have been the work of days at the hands of skilled printers. Graphics packages offer enormous possibilities of choice and manipulation of images to graphic designers; and spreadsheet programs enable a computer to model situations involving numeric data.

On the face of it, computer technology seems to confer only benefits on business practice. A company can tap into vast databases, or seek the help of an 'expert system'. It can file information, and access that information, with unprecedented accuracy and speed. It can keep better records, refine its accounting methods, present information and communicate more efficiently and more impressively than ever before. By way of example, the work of even quite small travel agents has been 'revolutionised' by the possibilities of on-line multi-access systems: tickets can be booked almost instantaneously, and data and money can be transferred electronically, thus obviating the need for paper and cash transactions.

Computer technology has created many new jobs for hardware and software producers, systems analysts, programmers and maintenance engineers — but many jobs have been lost as well. Typists, typesetters, filing clerks, bank employees (made redundant by automated cash machines, for example) are just some of the victims. And it is not only low-level jobs that have been lost: when human expertise is encoded — when computers can give financial advice of higher quality than individual experts can — those experts are rendered superfluous. Who needs a stockbroker when shares can be bought and sold by computer? Solicitors, too, may feel the draught as divorcing couples turn for legal advice to the Internet. And the nature of the job for those in work is changing: it consists of long hours in front of a VDU, whose consequences may be boredom, fatigue and (allegedly) repetitive strain injury. The work that they do and the speed at which they do it may well be closely monitored, too, by the very computers that they are paid to operate.

Position B: some unfortunate consequences of these developments

> Finally, small businesses, unable to afford ever-developing computer systems, may be casualties in competition with transnational companies that can. There may be as much menace in the globalisation of business that computer technology has made possible, as there is promise.

Conclusion: a balanced view

e This is a subject on which many a student is better informed than many a teacher. My answer is a conventional one, and it is the product of no more than a layperson's reading of the national press. I do give some examples, but I should have felt more comfortable if I had been able to give one or two more.

A04 Like so many other 'science and technology' essay titles, you are invited here to reach an open verdict — or perhaps to find some negative effects of a technological advance. There can be few developments in science and technology that do not carry with them unfortunate side-effects.

As ever, *opinions* must be based on *evidence*; but so many promises were made concerning the 'wired society' that a little scepticism is in order. If knowledge has its *limitations*, so too does information.